# Women in America

**FROM COLONIAL TIMES TO THE 20TH CENTURY**

# Women in America

## FROM COLONIAL TIMES TO THE 20TH CENTURY

*Advisory Editors*
LEON STEIN
ANNETTE K. BAXTER

*A Note About This Volume*

What of the women behind the men at Valley Forge? Walter H. Blumenthal has combed through records of orderlies, expense and ration accounts, and other primary sources preserved from the time of the American Revolution. He has gathered together the bits of information, the revealing written notes, the entries in diaries and bulletins that together create a picture that touches the heart and reprimands history. There were women on both sides of the conflict that followed the men into bloody battle lines and bitter winter weather. Some were drawn by love, others by hunger. At a time when hope was drained on the American side and imperial authority had been stopped on the other, they came to the camps to wash, to clean, to cook, to provide companionship—some in sin and some in devotion—while more comfortable citizens continued at a safe distance business as usual. This is their footnote in history.

# Women Camp Followers

## OF THE

# American Revolution

WALTER HART BLUMENTHAL

## ARNO PRESS

*A New York Times Company*
NEW YORK – 1974

Reprint Edition 1974 by Arno Press Inc.

Reprinted from a copy in The State
  Historical Society of Wisconsin Library

WOMEN IN AMERICA
From Colonial Times to the 20th Century
ISBN for complete set: 0-405-06070-X
See last pages of this volume for titles.

Manufactured in the United States of America

Library of Congress Cataloging in Publication Data

Blumenthal, Walter Hart, 1883-1969.
  Women camp followers of the American Revolution.

  (Women in America:  from colonial times to the 20th
century)
  Reprint of the ed. published by G. S. MacManus
Co., Philadelphia.
  Bibliography:  p.
  1.  United States--History--Revolution, 1775-1783
--Women.  2.  Camp followers.  I.  Title.  II.  Series.
E276.B55  1974       973.3'3      74-3931
ISBN 0-405-06077-7

# WOMEN CAMP FOLLOWERS
# OF THE
# AMERICAN REVOLUTION

# Women Camp Followers

## OF THE

# American Revolution

BY

WALTER HART BLUMENTHAL

Philadelphia
GEORGE S. MacMANUS COMPANY
1952

PRINTED IN THE UNITED STATES OF AMERICA
PRESS OF GEORGE S. FERGUSON COMPANY
PHILADELPHIA, PA.

To Two Old Friends
Dr. Samuel Leopold
and
Walter L. Rosemont

## FOREWORD

*The subject here presented never has been set forth in a comprehensive inquiry. Not so much as one covering article is known to our research. Except in cursory paragraphs and allusions, this aspect of the War for Independence has been neglected. Yet, the presence of women camp followers, on the ration or otherwise, was a salient factor of those years of military struggle and forsaken homes.*

*Every effort has been made to garner the facts fully and to recount them without bias or animus. But since the British soldiery were called 'redcoats' by the patriots, we so term them in our text, as also the Hessians as hirelings, which they were, though not of their own volition. Moreover, if many of the feminine camp companions of the king's troopers were wives only on the ration rolls, and perhaps some among the Americans, that does not lessen the service they rendered their men in the drudgery of campaign and bivouac.*

*Remote now seem those heroic days when nationhood was won; forgotten the names of those wives and sweethearts who ministered to their men in the field or tended home and harvest, abiding the hoped-for return. These men and women alike ventured their all for independence from the overseas thrall. May the liberties under law they achieved in that ordeal of long ago be forever cherished by those to whom America is the signet of freedom.*

*W. H. B.*

# CONTENTS

# BRITISH CAMP WOMEN
## ON THE RATION

# BRITISH CAMP WOMEN ON THE RATION

THAT both England and America had women camp followers in the seven years' struggle of the Thirteen Colonies for self-government has never been fully presented. Except for wives of officers, these contingents belonged with the baggage, and in military orders are not infrequently so mentioned. The British historian of the American Revolution, Henry Belcher, admits that "swarms of prostitutes followed the British forces, as they have other armies in all their campaigns." [1]

Though there was usually an allotted number of wives and alleged wives permitted to each British regiment by the military commanders, and transported overseas with these troops, no certainty prevailed as to the marital status of many, and the number of women so allotted was often exceeded by those subsequently gathered by the forces along the way and in garrison. Since these latter might not receive rations, such camp followers, picked up by detachments on the march or in encampment with the passing months, through the necessity of foraging encumbered the army more than did those brought from overseas.

Thus Lord George Germain, British Secretary of State for America, early in the American War for Independence assigned eight regiments to put down the 'rebellion.' Expecting only brief hostilities with the provincials, these sailed in January, 1776, and with officers consisted of 677 men each, sixty women each, and a dozen servants. Soon thereafter his lordship ordered a detachment from Jamaica consisting of 374 officers and men, forty women, and servants. Next month he despatched the 42nd Highlanders with 1,168 officers and men and eighty women, followed by Fraser's Corps of 2,298 fighting men and 160 women.[2]

Six months after Lexington, with the surrender of the little garrison of 300 Canadians at Chambly on the Sorel River (north of Lake Champlain), General Richard Montgomery wrote, October 20, 1775, to General Philip Schuyler concerning the five precious tons of powder captured, and added: "Their number of women and quantity of baggage is astonishing"; though how many women there were with this small force he did not specify. The story was the same at the taking of Ticonderoga, and the Hessian General Friedrich von Wurmb wrote on one occasion from Newport, "The fact is that this corps has more women and children than men, which causes considerable vexation."

At the British evacuation of Boston, March 17, 1776, the 22nd Regiment had attached 87 women, 61 children; the 25th, 80 women, 49 children; the 40th, 107 women, 85 children; the 43rd, 92 women, 71 children; the 52nd, 84 women, 100 children; the 63rd, 96 women, 64 children; and the Artillery, 121 women, 123 children.[3] This incomplete list aggregated 667 women and 553 children, attached to fewer than half the departing troops.

There is meager evidence that several of the various contingents of German mercenaries brought women with them by authorization. It is significant that on June 1, 1777, there were, for example, 4,301 Brunswick hired troops on the payroll, the tabulation including officers, non-commisisoned officers, privates, musicians, servants, but no mention of rationed women since they received no pay; whereas we learn from an earlier manuscript muster that on March 17, 1776 (the day Boston was evacuated by the British), sixteen English vessels bore the First Division of Brunswickers from Stade, near Hamburg on the Elbe; that they comprised 77 women and 2,290 men, of whom 1,680 were privates, 50 drummers, 85 corporals, 139 orderlies, teamsters and others.[4] This documentary Return is one of only three or four such evidences showing women brought with the mercenaries from the point of embarkation. With one Corps six were permitted to a company.[5] Colonel Charles Rainsford, as commissary for embarking foreign troops in the English service from Germany, lists 60 women with the 1,285 Anspach troops who came down the Rhine, and 15 women with a contingent of 423 Hanau infantry.[6] There is further mention of "Women and Baggage" in these muster rolls.

Fortunately, we may herewith present the figures of Daniel Wier, commissary to the British Army in America, insofar as they pertain to our inquiry. These reveal the number of rationed women and children early in the war, and afford a basis of comparison with the figures hereinafter given for a date two months prior to the surrender of Cornwallis and the virtual cessation of hostilities.

The report of Wier, dated May 20, 1777, at New York, transmits statistical Returns to John Robinson, Esq., Secretary to the Lords Commissioners of the Treasury. The commissary writes that the victualling transports from Cork had arrived, and that on one of the returning ships he is sending with this letter an inventory of army stores on hand, together with the number of British and German forces daily victualled, which is 36,000, including waggoners, boatmen, skinners, women at half count, children at quarter, and 500 rebel prisoners. He adds:

"In the computation is included the Women and Children belonging to each Regiment, which are indeed very numerous beyond any Idea of imagination; and although the former are victualled at the rate of a moiety of each man's allowance, and the latter at a fourth only, yet the expence is very considerable. As it is my Duty as well as my inclination, to reduce this, as well as every other extraordinary expence, consistent with propriety and humanity, I hope we shall be able, with the advice and concurrence of the General, to adopt some plan in order to curtail in some degree this enormous Expence." [7]

For the British forces the Commissary's figures are listed under some forty regimental and battalion headings, and with the several civil department branches (omitting prisoners), total 23,101 men, 2,776 women, 1,904 children. The Germans, under sixteen corps headings, total 11,192 men, 381 women, with children not listed. In this aggregation of 3,157 women the ratio to men among the British was about one to eight; among the Germans about one to thirty.

The figures are available of the British and Foreign (Hessian *et al*) forces, and civil departments of their dual army, victualled at New York and outposts, August 22, 1781. These show a grand total of 23,489 men, 3,615 women, 4,127 children. The British regiments comprise 9,686 men and 2,173 women, the Germanic regiments 10,251 men and 679 women, the civil departments (Quartermaster, Commissary, Engineer, Hospital, Barrack, Boatmen personnel) 3,512 men and 763 women.[8]

It will be noted that the proportion among the British troops was about one to every four and a half, whereas the mercenaries numbered fifteen men to one woman. Thus the four-year interval had doubled the feminine ratio—doubtless largely by wayside accretion. In the above summarized New York area Return for 1781 we note as typical the British 17th Dragoons with 389 men, 103 women, as compared with the 3rd Waldeck mercenaries with 385 men, 24 women; the Jersey Volunteers with 582 men, 179 women, the Hessian Yagers with 831 men, 88 women; the 42nd British Regiment with 701 men, 110 women, as compared with the Hessian Hanau Volunteers with 755 men, 65 women.

Muster Returns of mercenaries for later years sometimes included women—obviously married or consorted with during military service here, in addition to those brought over. Thus, after peace, the few German detachments in Canada, sailing home from Quebec, numbered 105 officers, 1,776 men, and 64 women.[9] Of the total of 29,867 such mercenaries sent over to America, some 5,000 deserted or refused to return home, while 7,554 were killed or died of wounds, illness, or accident. (Among those who deserted were many who were accompanied by women.)

If some of the German contingents came without women, it may be inferred that as the campaigns dragged on through the years these regiments, irked by knowledge of the British female quotas, were placated by possible importations. Even though confirmation of this supposition may not be available in readily accessible sources (such as the Clinton MSS. in the Wm. L. Clements Library), scrutiny of unpublished data in the Treasury and Audit Office Papers of transport payments for the period in the British Public Record Office might reveal such a shipment. We are here on debatable ground; but certain it is that there was no condign moral reprobation to balk such sending of women. "The standard of morality in the army did not rise higher than that if the age." For seven years Hessians had permanent garrisons at Brooklyn and roundabout.

The unproved theory of the so-called Jackson-Whites of the Ramapo region, allegedly harking back to an importation of women by a contractor named Jackson for the Hessians, under British authority, is wholly hypothetical. Among these mercenaries the ratio of women, as we have seen, was one to thirty men in 1777, and one to fifteen in 1781. That women permitted with Hessian, Brunswick, and Waldeck contingents by authorization came in the same ships as the troops is unlikely, for the mercenaries—many of them striplings under twenty—were sometimes sent to sea by the British Quartermaster Department packed aboard in such cramped quarters that six were put in sleeping bunks intended for four, so that "the whole file would turn over at once." Some of the vermin-ridden ships bringing the first consignment were fourteen weeks in crossing from embarkation in Hanover.

Among British troops in the American War for Independence care of the sick and the wounded was of the crudest. Trained nursing was unknown, and Florence Nightingale's innovation was seventy years in the future. Women camp followers nursed their men (husbands or otherwise), or groups of such women were ordered to serve at improvised so-called field hospitals as occasion might require. Life was lightly held in the overseas military mentality and it was deemed cheaper "to levy a recruit than to cure a soldier." Medical provisions in the field were on a par with conditions on the older British man-of-war sailing vessels of the period, which might lack a sick-bay (or have a cubby without portholes), but which, as on the *Panther*, had a pigsty under the forecastle, and carried live sheep in a launch stowed on the main deck amidships.

As early as midsummer of 1775 a shipload of sixty widows and orphans of the slain, together with 170 amputee and invalided soldiers and officers, were embarked for England on the brig *Charming Nancy*. Though the wife of the General, Mistress Gage herself, sailed on this passage, the conditions aboard were abominable as usual in that day. That the distress was acute may be gleaned from a contemporary chronicle of their landfall, after 24 days, at Plymouth. The "Annual Register" comments on the emaciated scarecrow appearance of the men, and of the women and children declares: "Some of these too exhibited a most shocking spectacle; and even the vessel itself was almost intolerable from the stench arising from the sick and wounded." A collection was taken up in port for the benefit of the women and children and £100 distributed, before the ship sailed for the Thames where the men were sent to Chelsea Hospital.

Throughout the struggle, the companionate wives and others of the British soldiery cooked, washed and mended for their men as best they could. They were a recognized and mayhap needed element of the camps as then constituted, and consequently authorized quotas were rationed by the military authorities, who were at times even inclined to countenance feminine newcomers recruited by the men from the roadside, or petticoat stragglers from the town, giddied by the uniforms and drawn to the unfettered life of the open. Yet they were troublesome and indifferent to discipline, lagged behind or thrust themselves ahead in a march, plundered on the way, and were keen for illicit rum-traffic, always deeming too meager the quota dispensed by the commissary to all.

It was a hard drinking age; the standards of morality in the British ranks mirrored the period, and, as always under military conditions on enemy soil, tended to be lower. To augment the rum ration of the men, the women constantly gave trouble with clandestine liquor traffic. There were repeated British orders against camp women bringing in intoxicants. Somehow, the caliber of female camp followers with the American forces kept the Continentals more within bounds. As one authority notes:

"Both armies tried to keep their rum-selling in the hands of authorized sutlers. But the American problem was comparatively simple, since it was long before women attached themselves to the new force, there being in America no such slum-class as mostly supplied the women of the European armies." [10]

When the women with the British smuggled liquor from Boston to nearby Charlestown, General William Howe revoked their permission to go to the town. In Boston the women were in barracks, in the Charlestown encampment they were in huts and hutches where carousing prevailed. To lessen pilfering excursions, and possible arson, Howe ordered that army women should not be present "at any fires that may happen." He noted that "some Irregular Women" are encamped with his troops, and colonels are notified to permit only the allotted number of women per company.

Burgoyne issued an order at his camp near Ticonderoga, July 3, 1777, forbidding that liquor be either sold or given to "the Savages," and stating:

"Commanding Officers are to assemble the Sutlers and Women of the respective Regiments, and inform them that the first person found guilty of disobedience shall instantly have their liquors and sutling stores destroyed and [be] turned out of Camp, besides receiving such Corporal Punishment as a Court Martial shall inflict." [11]

Yet, the year before, rum was lushed out to the Indians with Burgoyne's army "without any Rule or Ration," a supply of 125,000 gallons having been shipped from the West Indies for them in 1776.

A fortnight after the above warning, the playboy General, at the lower end of Lake Champlain, issued another order against "vending of Spirituous Liquors by the Sutlers or any other followers of the army . . . to Soldiers, Women or Savages," and requiring officers to "examine all Huts, Tents, or other abodes in the rear of the Encampment," any offenders to be taken prisoner and the liquor "belonging to him or her destroyed, and burn the dwelling." [12]

The staggering amount of rationed rum did not suffice the redcoats, and the supplementary illicit traffic was limited only by the pittance of pay of the troopers. The Commissary General's Department reported to British headquarters at New York that from June 1, 1778, to June 30, 1781, £359,573 was paid for 1,595,775 gallons! This was about three times the sum paid during these three years for beef and pork, bread and flour together. Things were not going so well in 1780, and that year £152,878 was expended for 643,828 gallons of solace—or about a pint a day per man, if the mercenaries got their share. No wonder the Commissary mentions rum as "the most considerable expence" among supplies. And in consumption, the camp women assisted the warriors.

It is therefore understandable why that British authority on this war, Belcher, states: "There followed Burgoyne's army, as was computed, about 2,000 women, of whom 300 were on the strength of the regiments, while the rest were fed and maintained by the soldiers themselves. It would seem as if all warriors of the correct model went on campaign with sword in one hand, a lass on the disengaged arm, and a bottle knocking up against his cartridge box rearwards." [13]

Burgoyne's forces had numbered above 8,000; one MS. Return states 5,791 surrendered at Saratoga, of whom 2,431 were Germans. The camp followers are not enumerated. Though the future author of comedies denied he had such a legion of women in his train, his personal amours lend color to the allegation. Howe, likewise, frittered time in the arms of his mistress; and hearsay charges, perhaps unfounded, were also rife concerning General Sir Henry Clinton, who twice dallied in New York while a British army was surrounded and captured.

An inquiry concerning the conduct of the war came up before a committee of the House of Commons in 1779. On cross examination, Colonel Kingston naïvely averred, concerning the Burgoyne forces, he "did not know that there were many women followed the army; he had no time to attend to their beauty or their numbers; he never heard there were 2,000, nor did he believe there were half that number."

On further questioning, the Colonel answered that "there were only three women allowed to every company; that provisions were allowed for so many and no more; that the Commissary, without a gross breach of his duty, could not issue any more rations than what the order allowed; and, as for impeding the baggage, it was impossible, for if any more women than were allowed by the order attended, they must have walked, or found a mode of carriage for themselves." [14]

Concerning the huge drove of women with Burgoyne's unlucky expedition from Canada in 1777, we are on safe ground in quoting Belcher, who states:

"Most of these poor outcasts must have perished miserably after the capture of the British force at Saratoga. It is obvious that in marching through any country, however friendly it might be to the King's cause, camp followers of this class, who are ever on the edge of destitution, maraud and purloin and behave with outrage. They would take a fierce pleasure in annoying and insulting the prudent and decent women of cottages and farms adjacent to their line of march. The pillage and robbery of Loyalists and their homes in Jersey and in Westchester were largely due to this band of loose women, which was largely recruited from local sources  Nor did this plague of women affect only the men in the ranks. The commander-in-chief and some of the divisional generals at least set the example; their ladies, who were other men's wives, and as well known as uniform buttons, gambled and swore and drank; but these women were not imported from Great Britain." [15]

It would be difficult to say in how far they were "from local sources"; but the American forces were comparatively free from depraved hangers-on. Belcher, noting how the efficiency of the overseas army was impaired, adds: "There is no means of computing the crippling effect on Howe's army of vice and plagues, from which the American field forces were probably delivered."

We are given a picture of these captured Burgoyne troops, with their women, in the words of an intelligent feminine American who saw them march by her home at Cambridge. It was not an edifying spectacle, as Hannah Winthrop described it in her letter to Mercy Warren. The letter is dated November 11, 1777, less than a month after Burgoyne had capitulated at Saratoga. Washington was with his ragged and hungry men at White Marsh, near Philadelphia. That very day he wrote to the President of Congress from White Marsh camp, pleading the "want of cloaths and Blankets, and the little prospect we have of obtaining relief."

Here in part is Hannah Winthrop's missive in its original spelling:

"Last thursday, a large number of British troops came softly thro the Town [Cambridge] via Watertown to Prospect hill. on Friday we heard the Hessians were to make a Procession in the same rout, we thot we should have nothing to do with them, but View them as they Passt. To be sure the sight was truly astonishing. I never had the least Idea that the Creation produced such a sordid set of creatures in human Figure—poor, dirty, emaciated men, great numbers of women, who seemed to be the beasts of burthen, having a bushel basket on their back, by which they were bent double, the contents seemed to be Pots and Kettles, various sorts of Furniture, children peeping thro' gridirons and other utensils, some very young Infants who were born on the road, the women bare feet, cloathed in dirty rags, such effluvia filld the air while they were passing, had they not been smoaking all the time, I should have been apprehensive of being contaminated by them. After a noble looking advancd Guard Gen. J - - y B[urgoy]n headed this terrible group on horseback. The other G[enera]l also, cloathd in Blue Cloaks. Hessians, Anspachers, Brunswickers, etc., followed on. The Hessian G[enera]l gave us a Polite Bow as they Passd. Not so the British. their Baggage Waggons drawn by poor half starvd horses. But to bring up the rear, another fine Noble looking Guard of American Brawny Victorious Yeomanry, who assisted in bringing these sons of slavery to terms, some of our Waggons drawn by fat oxen, driven by joyous looking Yankees closd the cavalcade." [16]

Many of them barefooted in mid-November, the bedraggled women went through Cambridge and, as Hannah Winthrop continues, the woebegone ranks of females and soldiers "trudged thro thick and thin to the hills, where we thot they were to be confined, but what was our Surprise when in the morning we beheld an inundation of these disagreeable objects filling our streets!" Some had been three weeks on the way from Saratoga, where on ground to the east the women and children had huddled with the detached sick and wounded.

Regarding the number of women with Burgoyne's army, the statement of Belcher is significant concerning the alleged horde of 2,000 (presumably fewer), that only "300 were on the strength of the regiments, while the rest were fed and maintained by the soldiers themselves."

After the surrender at Saratoga the capitulated troops had been marched some 200 miles in thirteen days and upwards to the vicinity of Cambridge—men, women and children sleeping in the open during the frosty nights. The downcast British were put in makeshift sheds on Prospect Hill, the doltish Hessians on Winter Hill. Snow drifted in at the open sides. Sergeant Roger Lamb, who was there, bitterly declares, with possible exaggeration: "It was not infrequent for thirty or forty persons, men, women and children, to be indiscriminately crowded together in one small, miserable, open hut; a scanty portion of straw their bed, their own blankets their only covering." [17]

A Return of the British prisoners who drew rations at Prospect Hill, November 22, 1777, gives 215 women; while a Provision Return of the mercenaries gives 82 women—a total of 297, exclusive of officers' wives quartered with Burgoyne at Cambridge a month after his surrender.[18] Since, according to General Horatio Gates, *872 officers* and 4,991 rank and file were surrendered (including the British, German, and Canadian forces), there were doubtless scores of women attached to the huge contingent of officers. Besides anonymous ladies there were Madame de Riedesel with her young family and maid; Lady Harriet Acland and maid; also the wellbred wife of Major Henry Harmage who was seriously wounded, and gentle Anne Reynal, wife of Lieut. Thomas Reynal who was killed in the fighting preceding the surrender.

The wife of General Riedesel in 1777 had followed her husband across the ocean to Quebec with her three children, the firstborn five years of age, the youngest an infant. She brought along a large stock of wine for the Baron's consumption, and accompanied him on Burgoyne's campaign with two maid-servants, a calash and horses. Her Hessian husband headed the German contingent in the expedition from Canada. Two children were born during and subsequent to the campaign and were named Canada and America, though not out of love for the New World, for the comments in her "Letters and Journals" are disparaging and typically Teutonic. Therein she writes of Boston that the women regarded her with repugnance and even spat at her as she passed.

But besides the officers' ladies, or their "ammunition wives," there was the raggle-taggle of female followers of the file. The American General William Heath, responsible for the Saratoga prisoners, bridled in Boston because, despite his orders, venturesome internees in pilfered garb got through his chain of sentries into the town, and their women strolled in the streets of Cambridge.

When Congress after a year ordered the Burgoyne prisoners to be marched in winter on meager rations from Massachusetts to Virginia, General Washington had the humanity to order wagons for the women and children.[19] Invalided officers having families with them were permitted to go by ship to the James River. Burgoyne and his staff had been allowed to return to England on parole.

On their 700-mile trudge southward, the docile soldiery, seemingly unguarded and unguided, plodded
through the Berkshires, the Hudson Highlands, New
Jersey, slept in the patriots' abandoned huts at Valley
Forge on the way to Lancaster, and crossed the Susque-
hanna at Yorktown. Maryland by show of arms opposed
the entrance of the clomping stragglers across her bor-
ders. Having left Cambridge on November 10, 1778,
the Convention troops, as they were called, reached the
assigned encampment at Charlotteville on January 16.

On the way 400 deserted, some with their female
companions. Such desertions were regarded with indif-
ference by the sore beset patriots, who permitted the
procession to wend its way with only desultory direc-
tion. Others took up new helpmates on the wayside,
and the ranks reaching Virginia remained prisoners
until the peace, save those who died or escaped. Among
the Germans who deserted on the journey southward
many took American wives [20] and founded families that
grew to respected citizenship. A Hessian officer wrote
during the wayfare: "At all the places through which
we passed dozens of girls were met with on the road,
who either laughed at us mockingly, or now and then
roguishly offered us an apple . . . the fair sex were
the cause of our losing some of our comrades. . . ." [21]

In localities where other Hessian contingents had
fought and marauded in earlier sortees, these Burgoyne
mercenaries met with hostility on their march; elsewhere with lukewarm doles. Around Lancaster the
buxom Pennsylvania-German girls were not too friendly.
But German sectarian settlers in remoter areas were

cordial to the point of offering their daughters as wives to such as would stay behind.[22] At Valley Forge the foreign marchers met with hatred, the housewives refusing food "handouts" to all except women and children. The Hessians spent Christmas Eve encamped in that vicinity, bought liquor from settlers willing to sell, and a drunken carouse ensued in which the women began to fight. We are told the men took sides in the fracas and the fighting became riotous. "The guard was called, but as soon as they left the fight was resumed and continued well into the night." [23]

Most of the mercenaries were of conscript character, caught in the dragnet spread by German princelings to replenish depleted coffers. Many were robust, fine fellows. But 19-year-old Charles Augustus of Saxe-Weimar refused to permit any of his subjects to be dragooned for overseas vassal service except vagabonds and convicts. The Prince Charles contingent numbered 582 men and 21 women in a count on November 25, 1776.

Madame de Riedesel records with rankled hauteur that on her peregrination south in a Canadian calash with her children and two female attendants the inhabitants more than once refused to sell food to Madame General, Baroness Friederike Charlotte Louise Riedesel. The captured troops on their arrival had found the barracks unfinished and the ration of meat inedible. About the middle of February, Madame de Riedesel and her three peaked little girls joined the now moody Hessian Major General who had rented a fine estate and manorial home near Monticello. The Baroness complained of rattlesnakes, thunderstorms, and the heat, but failed in her memoirs to mention Jefferson, who accorded them and other Hessian officers his urban hospitality. Madame had her fifth girl child here, and Jefferson on May 13, 1780, sent playful condolences on the birth of another daughter.

In that march southward to Virginia in the winter of 1778-9, there had been in all 4,459 British and Hessian prisoners of war—2,577 of the former, 1,882 of the latter. The three aggregations of mercenaries under Baron Riedesel had crossed the Hudson at Fishkill a few days after the British, likewise in three contingents, were ferried over. The three British groups reached York on December 16-19. The first division of Germans arrived there on December 22, and numbered 949. With this body were a large number of women and children, transported in wagons.

Because of the threat of Cornwallis's army, the Convention prisoners were ordered moved northward from Charlottesville to Pennsylvania in May, 1781. Under militia escort, they arrived at Lancaster early in June and were shunted about in nearby towns. The British were for a time quartered in barracks near Lancaster and York, and the Germans at Reading. On June 17, Major Bailey conducted from York two divisions, one of about 1,000 mercenaries, to Reading, and another of 900, "with about 300 women and children," to Lancaster.[24] There were thus among the Germans almost one-sixth as many women and children as men. It will be recalled that in the Daniel Wier Return of

May 20, 1777, the proportion of women among the hirelings was one to thirty.

Meanwhile, Burgoyne, back in England was not chastened by his American defeat, but flourished as a playwright. His wife, Lady Charlotte, having died during his American campaigns, he took an opera singer, Susan Caulfield, as mistress. He had four children by her in the decade of this affair that ended with his death, one of these offspring as an adult becoming a British field marshal. But Gentleman Johnny was buried beside his wife, at his own behest, beneath an ungraven slab in Westminster Abbey. So dashing a figure in life—today the exact spot of his interment is said to be unknown.

Concerning Burgoyne and Howe, the charge that they idled precious time with the wives of complaisant subordinate officers seems borne out by the lax moral tone of the former's staff, and the notorious affair of Howe with Mrs. Joshua Loring, whose unsavory husband he gave the lucrative post of Commissary General of Prisoners.

( It cannot be laid to spite that Madame de Riedesel in her memoirs accuses Burgoyne of seeking almost nightly oblivion in drink toward the close of the Saratoga campaign, and of "amusing himself with the wife of a commissary, who was his mistress."[25] (Eelking says he always had a good cook and usually a mistress. That both Burgoyne and Howe so lapsed in the face of disaster was bad military conduct, whatever the moral aspect. )

(The perfumed Loyalist lady, Mrs. Loring, shared Howe's tastes, both being proficient at drinking and gambling.) Known as 'the sultana' to the officers, she accompanied his army through the three years of his dawdling campaigns. "They used to drink all day and all evening. . . . The success of American arms undoubtedly owed a heavy debt to the success of hers," declares one historian. And a contemporary critic asked: "What do you think of the favorite sultana losing 300 guineas in a night at cards, who three years ago would have found it difficult to have mustered as many pence?" [26] She had been a Miss Lloyd, married to 25-year-old Loring in 1769 at the house of Colonel Nathaniel Hatch, in Dorchester, Massachusetts. A son, Henry, died in 1832, Archdeacon of Calcutta.

The Bostonian Tory husband of Mrs. Loring, in the appointment he secured through her influence, reaped a corrupt income by appropriating and selling nearly two-thirds of the rations allowed patriot prisoners, thereby starving Americans by hundreds, as did Provost Marshal Cunningham in New York in the most vicious cruelty of the war.

This dallying by Howe is derided by Francis Hopkinson, one of the Signers, who wrote "Hail Columbia." In his risible "Battle of the Kegs" he wrote:

> Sir William, he, snug as a flee,
>   Lay all this time a-snoring,
> Nor dream'd of harm as he lay warm
>   In bed with Mrs. Loring.

Gambling among the British officers was such that many were ruined by high play, some being forced to sell their commissions to defray debts at 'pharo' and other games.

During the British occupation of Philadelphia in the Spring of 1778, twenty-three staff officers expended 3,300 guineas in the most elaborate fête champêtre ever given in colonial America, 750 of the city's Loyalist social set enjoying the costume ball, regatta, feast and fireworks. This 'Mischianza' of May 18 on Mr. Joseph Wharton's lawn overlooking the Delaware marked the recent arrival of Sir Henry Clinton and the farewell of Howe. But, a month later to the day, Clinton, on express orders from England, evacuated Philadelphia with 3,000 of the Loyalist inhabitants, marching northward through New Jersey, with the ill bound for New York on ships that sailed down the Delaware.

High officers of the German mercenaries were amazed at these British frivolities in Philadelphia, including theatricals by "Howe's Thespians." Thus General Friedrich von Wurmb wrote: "We have parties and gamble, whereby every night 700 and 800 pounds are lost and won. Gen. Howe also gambles. Each Monday there is a play. The actors are English officers and their mistresses." [27]

Whether most of the women who came overseas in the permitted regimental quotas were lawfully wedded is uncertain; but it was stated by Lieutenant Colonel Maunsell, who was in charge of embarkations at Cork, that it was essential to permit a certain number of women to accompany the troops bound for America to prevent desertions. That astute participant, Sergeant Roger Lamb, had taken unto himself another soldier's runaway wife, named Kate Harlowe, who bore him a child. He tells in his candid Memoir that a private, wishing to marry, was supposed to obtain written consent of an officer of his company, "as but few young women could be taken on board when the regiment embarked for foreign service." [28]

Laxity among the officers tends to confirm the suspicion that proof of wedlock was not required. Charles Stedman, who served as a British commissary, remarks how, during the occupation of Philadelphia, certain of the king's officers shocked staid Quakers and "some of the first families" by sometimes bringing their mistresses with them into the abodes where they were quartered.[29] There and elsewhere Tory daughters were wooed by redcoated officers, and many a dame and damsel caught 'scarlet fever' from the lobsterbacks, in patriot vernacular.

It is clear that the number of women carried by the Royal forces 'on the strength'—authorized and rationed quotas—was exceeded by attachments in the field and on the march, with resultant foraging forays on the way. It is hard to picture these incredible processions, with children sometimes born on the march. Howe, who permitted six women per company (of 38 men, nine officers) during his campaign of 1776 and 1777, must have condoned the excess over that number. In Burgoyne's invasion from Canada the quota was three per company, but, as Allen French states, "the number that actually went was scandalously high." Clinton stipulated at Mount Holly, June 20, 1778: "The Regiments to draw for their Women, at the rate of two per Company only."

Incredible, too, the neglect with which the British soldier of that period was still treated. With scant food allowance, and deplorable medical facilities, with deductions for clothing, the pay for infantry privates of 8d. to 1s.1d. per day, and that not in coin—indicates the conditions. The effort to put down the patriots was handled with astonishing ineptness. Witness the alleged British attempt to secure 20,000 mercenaries from Russia—and the opinion of General Howe, written July 7, 1777, to Lord George Germain (who, responsible in London for the conduct of the war, *forgot* to send to Howe the orders to cooperate with Burgoyne), that with "a Corps of Russians of 10,000 effective fighting Men I think I would insure the Success of the War to Great Britain in another campaign." There was even Parliamentary talk of sending 24,000 Moors as mercenaries, hired from the Fez of Morocco.

Imagine the prospect of vanquishing the stripling but determined colonials by Howe who finds time at Halifax, June 6, 1776, to order the Quartermasters of Artillery "to apply for the Women's and Children's Shoes and Stockings appropriated to those Regiments."

In keeping with the times, it was a strange and bungled effort to overcome the American struggle for freedom. A Parliamentary commission appointed in 1780 to investigate the finances of the overseas army ceased its inquiry in despair. A Return of March, 1779, shows that among the somewhat meager British forces (4,000 in December of that year) occupying then small New York, shelter had to be found for 1,550 women and their 968 children! [30] With the numerical strength of British regiments as likely to be under as over 500 men, we find as typical the famed Royal Artillery reported at New York in August, 1781, as comprising on the ration list 515 men, 133 women, and 120 children! And it may be taken for granted that wedlock was inferential only, though many wives of officers and men encumbered their husbands.

Various orders pertaining to such camp women indicate that their presence was troublesome rather than efficacious from the early days of the war onward. Eleven days before Bunker (Breed's) Hill, General Thomas Gage, who despite his American wife served the King, issued this order at Boston, June 6, 1775:

"Notwithstanding the care that has been taken to Provide the Women with proper places to stay in, some of them have broke into houses and Buildings that were infected with the Small Pox, by which there is Danger of its Spreading thro' the Town, Particularly a place that was shut up at the North end on Account of that Disorder, during the Winter. The Gen.l therefore desires the Off'rs Commanding Corps to have the Strictest enquiery immediately made, to discover the Women Concern'd, whom he is detirmined to order on Board Ship & Send away." [31]

General Sir William Howe, who superseded Gage four months after Bunker Hill, issued twenty-six admonitions concerning camp women.[32] We quote several to show their tenor:

At his Boston headquarters, June 20, 1775, he ordered:

"Two Women from each Corps to be sent to the General Hospital as soon as possible and four per Company to go to the Troops on the Charlestown side, the latter will be ordered to assemble on the Market Place at 2 o'Clock. A List of those Women to be given to a Serjeant who will attend to Conduct them to the Ferry, see them in the Boats and will be answerable that no more go than the Number Order'd."

At the camp on Charlestown Heights, June 22, 1775, Brigadier General Pigott ordered as spokesman for Howe:

"The Commanding Officers will be answerable the Number of Women with their respective Corps do's not exceed four per Company agreeable to the General Orders of the 20th that those be the best behaved and bring or keep no Children with them. If any Women are found in Camp Contrary to this Order they will be dismiss'd and sent Prisoners to Boston with Positive Directions not to be permitted to return from thence to this Camp."

Yet at this same camp a month later: "Some Irregular Women having been found in this Encampment, the Commanding Officers of Corps are requested to attend to the Order of June 20th. . . ."

At his Boston headquarters, October 14, 1775, Howe ordered:

"Women belonging to the Army convicted of selling Spiritous Liquors will be confined in the Provost till

there is an oppy of sending them away from hence."
Other orders linked rum and women in reproval, and
attempted restraint.

A week before the evacuation of Boston, he ordered, March 11, 1776:

"Any Woman belonging to the Army, that may be
found in Town after One O'Clock, will be taken up
and sent to the Provost and will be left behind."

On March 17, at four in the morning Howe's forces
of about 8,900 began their embarkation for Halifax,
with camp followers and more than 1,100 refugees.
In six hours they were all aboard 120 transports and
other craft, including sixteen armed vessels. On March
13, Howe's orders had read in part:

"The QrMasters of Corps to subsist their Women
and Children on board Ship, with Flour and Rice only,
till further Orders, and that it be issued to them with
Economy. A small Quantity of Fish may be given to
them with it. Each Corps to apply immediately at
No. 16 on the long Wharf for a Barrel of Salt Fish,
to be divided among the Men and Women."

Though he did not sail from Halifax for New York
until June 10, Howe on May 2 had ordered:

"Six Women per Company will be allow'd to embark
with each Regiment. The Commanding Officers will
be responsible that no more Women will be received
on board, nor any Children. Provisions will be allow'd
at the rate of half a Ration for each Woman, and one
quarter of a Ration for each Child, that is left behind."

Of the number of British and Irish women brought over as military wives with the English forces, augmented by campfire courtships over here, no accurate estimate is possible, though 5,000 during the period of the war may not be excessive. During the seven years of the war, Great Britain sent over in all fifty-one regiments of infantry, with a formal but variable strength of 477 each (comprising ten companies of 38 privates), and four battalions of artillery. Seventeen of the foot regiments served only in the earlier years. With the British total forces, after puny beginnings (there were 8,580 troops in America at the outbreak of the war), fluctuating between 19,000 and a peak of 31,000, and with the mercenaries averaging 17,000, this was no inconsiderable female assuagement for defeat.

During the year in which the British under Howe were cooped up in Boston the problem of food and fuel was acute for the soldiers, and their women and children, totaling 13,600. After Lexington and Concord, when these troops were first shut up in Boston, the population had been 6,753. Howe's military orders sought by severe measures to restrain what he termed the "profligacy and dissipation and want of subordination" of his forces. Flogging was common. The wife of a private who was detected as a receiver of stolen goods was sentenced to "one hundred lashes on her bare back, with a cat-o'-nine-tails, at the cart's tail, in different portions of the most conspicuous parts of the town, and to be imprisoned three months."

Infractions of discipline continued through the years of struggle. Other female followers of the overseas forces had backs bared to the bastinado for offenses deemed dire. General Henry Clinton demanded a count of the number of females "actually with each Corps," and ordered (Haddonfield, N. J., June 18, 1778) that:

"The Women of the Army are constantly to march upon the flanks of the Baggage of their respective Corps, and the Provost Martial has received positive Orders to Drum out any Woman who shall dare to disobey this Order." [33] On July 3 one was so drummed out after being lashed.

When Clinton heard of the French fleet approaching to blockade the Delaware, he evacuated Philadelphia. The royal army was ordered to withdraw by way of Brunswick, New Jersey, to Paulus Hook. At 3 o'clock in the morning of June 18, 1778, Sir Henry's cohort of 15,000 men and an immense baggage line marched forth, crossing the Delaware at Gloucester Point. Washington set out in pursuit from Valley Forge that same day.

Clinton's retreating army, in addition to British regulars and German auxiliaries, had Loyalist troops recruited in America, local Loyalist fleeing families, a huge aggregation of women and children camp followers on the ration, and straggling unattached nondescripts of both sexes. German and British soldiers had wooed and won many Palatinate girls and Philadelphia maidens, and throngs and clusters of these were in the procession. The whole plodding column and wagon cavalcade was twelve miles long. There was more confusion than discipline. Several hundred enlisted men or dragooned Hessians deserted on the march

(600 says Fortescue in his "History of the British Army"). Clinton issued a supplementary order that the women of each regiment should march in the vanguard, under escort of a non-commissioned officer and six men, who were to take care that the females "do not get out of the road on any account." This spectacle must have been a motley one, with possibly 1,500 women and as many children trudging ahead or begging a ride in the jouncing wagons.

Ten days later, the patriot forces under Washington came to grips with Clinton's army in the Battle of Monmouth. The torrid day and heat prostrations took almost as much toll as musket fire. The Colonials had 70 killed and 161 wounded; the British reported 65 killed and 170 wounded. Monmouth was the last pitched battle in the northern colonies. Thereafter the War was waged to the south.

One may wryly smile at the thought that Captain James A. Gardner in his salty recollections cited the loss of *baggage* before *women* when he tells us that in 1782, off Gibraltar, in an encounter with the French fleet, one of a convoy under Lord Howe was captured "with the baggage and the soldiers' wives, the only loss sustained." [34] Curiously, Belcher mentions such a whole shipload of women captured by the French off Gibraltar in 1784—"women from Castlerag and the Hard" (nautical limbo) —and follows with the dubious statement: "They were allowed on board the transports conveying the expeditionary force to America." [35]

Ladies of quality on shipboard sometimes gave rise to predicaments. When the British fleet was in the

Delaware, Captain John Barry conveyed ashore a covey of officers' ladies from aboard a captured vessel and entrusted them to Brigadier General William Small-wood at Wilmington. The latter in a quandary addressed General Washington, on March 16, 1778, asking what to do with his quarry of gentlewomen, with the result that arrangements were made to defray the bed and board cost of their accommodations.

Digressing now from the years of the Revolution, a presentation of our theme is required as it pertained to the earlier imperial struggle between France and England for American dominion.

Indeed, there was British precedent over here of women with the forces, for a score years before the Declaration a feminine contingent was conveyed from England with Braddock's command at the outset of the French and Indian War (1754-60). Many women accompanied Braddock's own force to the camp at Fort Cumberland, there to be augmented by further forces and camp followers. Colonel George Croghan had brought to camp along with some Iroquois allies a bevy of squaws and dusky maidens, who were soon to make such scandalous commotion among the British officers as to be ordered out of camp.[36]

In the earliest allusion to women with the Braddock strength we have a curious version of the possibly first sit-down strike! The order at Alexandria, April 7, 1755, reads:

"A greater number of Women having been brought over than those allowed by the Government sufficient for washing with a view that the Hospital might be servd; and complaint being made that a concert is entered into not to serve with out exorbitant Wages a Return will be called for of those who shall refuse to serve for six pence per day and their Provisions that they may be turned out of camp and others got in their places." [37]

If *others* would suffice, the idea that most were wives of the troopers would seem more or less a figment. Then as later the marital status of the feminine detachment was what might be termed relaxed. As one retrospect has it: ". . . most surely present of all were the women—sometimes wives of officers and soldiers, but more often not." Or as another puts it: "They were washerwomen, the wives and mistresses of common soldiers, good faithful women as well as common trulls who were apt to make trouble, get drunk and shift their partners."

The tattle that Braddock had brought two young women from England to dispel his loneliness in this barbarous land may have been baseless, but at Alexandria a twain named Mrs. Wardrope and Mrs. Spearing helped to amuse the General.[38]

Three weeks before departure, Braddock ordered on May 18:

"Six women per company are allowed to each of the two Regim'ts and the Independent companys; Four Women to each of the companys of carpenters of Virginia and Maryland Rangers; five women to the troop of Light Horse, as many to the detachment of seamen, and five to the detachment of artillery. His Excellency expects that this order will be punctually complied with, as no more Provsn will be allowed to be drawn for than for the above number of women." [39]

The day before Braddock set out from Fort Cumberland on his ill-fated march toward Fort Duquesne he decided to rid himself of some female encumbrance, and wrote, June 9, 1755, to Lieut.-Governor Robert H. Morris stating that these women's names had been listed (there were twenty-eight), and asking that the consignment be subsisted by the Pennsylvania government.[40]

That the women on the Braddock march were numerous despite those left behind may be judged from his order of June 11, one day out from Cumberland:

"No more than two Women per company to be allowed to march from the Camp, a List of the names of those that are to be sent back to be given into Capt. [Roger] Morris that there may be an Order sent to Col. [James] Innes at Fort Cumberland to Victual them. A List of the names of the women that are allowed to stay with the troops to be given in to the Major of Brigade and any woman that is found in camp and whose name is not in that List will for the first time be severely punished and for the second suffer Death." [41]

Several of the women permitted to go along were slain and scalped at the débacle, July 9, and three or more were made prisoners (the French Commander kept one for himself at Venango on the Allegheny, and sent two to Canada to be sold).[42]

When a force settled down in winter camp to the north it was observed that many semi-attached women vanished before the New England snows set in. In summer, on the contrary, they were frequently obstructive to military objectives and defense. When the French under Montcalm captured Oswego from the British, on August 14, 1756, there were in the English garrison among the officers and troops more than one hundred women and children. The women screamed for an end of hostilities, besought the defenders to run up a white flag, and thus hastened the surrender by their clamor.

Some of the hangers-on then and later were indentured female servants, runaways or those who had served their time, and who as often as not were "passed about a bit." [43] If an indentured woman was to be wed, the groom must buy her indenture. Some of these demi-slaveys were in wretched plight. Difficulties arose over these women, as in the following instance. There was a camp broil over an indentured woman taken by Captain Peter Hog who had been directed by the alarmed Virginia Assembly to build forts on the Virginia frontier after Braddock's defeat. The Assembly had voted £40,000 for the defence against the French and Indians, and the Virginia regiment was augmented to sixteen companies and the command given to Colonel George Washington. Captain Hog was rebuked for having appropriated one Joseph Chew's indentured girl without paying her master the value of the indenture. In his letter of rebuke Washington enclosed a dun-note from Chew, and Hog (having had the trull in camp for nine months), sent the £10 owed for the indenture.

Another sidelight concerns an army wife named Martha May, who after dereliction appeals for pardon. She wrote from Carlisle gaol, where her husband was confined for cause, and she likewise, for having thereafter abused Colonel Henry Bouquet. Addressing Bouquet, June 4, 1758, with abject apologies, she concludes: "I have been a Wife 22 years to have traveld with my Husband every Place or Country the Company marcht too and have workt very hard ever since I was in the Army. I hope yr Honour will be so good as to Pardon me this onct time that I may go with my Poor Husband one time more to carry him and my good Officers water in ye Hottest Battle as I have done before. Yr unfortunate Petitioner and Humble Servant, Martha May."[44]

Though six women per company was the usual quota in the field at the time, this was sometimes exceeded. Lt. Governor Robert Dinwiddie had complained of the excessive number encumbering some of the sixteen companies assigned to Washington, thereby exceeding the quota without the latter's knowledge.

Dinwiddie on May 26, 1757, ordered Lt.-Colonel Adam Stephen to proceed by sea on two sloops via Hampton Roads to South Carolina with two companies of one hundred men each under his command. Stephen was so assigned to protect South Carolina against the Creek Indians. (He was later to become Major General in the Continental service.) Stephen's subsequent Return reported 177 men taken instead of the 200 ordered. Concerning this discrepancy, Dinwiddie wrote Stephen, July 22:

"I can't tell how to reconcile this unless contrary to orders you carri'd more Women than I directed; the Number to a Company in all the Regulars are only six to a Comp'y, and you promis'd me to carry no more." [45]

The ferocious fighting of the French and Indian War, in which scalping was condoned by both sides, seldom had lighter interludes in festive spirit, although French officers at desolate outposts sought to teach the gavotte and quadrille to the Indian women of red allies. Occasions were rare when, at the more important strongholds, the temporary presence of ladies of quality afforded officers a respite from the campaign.

Quebec fell to the British on September 18, 1759. During the siege of July and August there were several brief truces in which the French and English exchanged civilities. General James Wolfe had sent several casks of wine to the French officers, and they responded with vintage. Hostilities were again suspended on July 22, while a party of French ladies, who had been captured by the besiegers the day before, were escorted into the citadel by Wolfe's aide-de-camp, Captain Hervey Smith. A French officer who was a participant in these amenities recounts in his Journal that all the women, though of differing rank, spoke well of the treatment they had received from the English officers. Several of them told of having supped with Wolfe, who had twitted them concerning the amatory restraint of his staff. In military parlance he jested that he had afforded favorable opportunities for romantic attack, but was chagrined that no advantage had been taken by his officers of such challenges to gallantry.

Even after the fall of Quebec, the humdrum routine of the victor ranks went on until the surrender of Montreal a year later. At nearby Point Levis a church had been converted into a hospital for the sick and wounded of the fleet. A British bulletin of February 25, 1760, stipulated: "The women belonging to the troops are now ordered to be victualled at four full rations for six, which is the number that each company, throughout the whole, are to Return and draw for." From first to last during those seven years of imperial struggle, women had helped or encumbered the combatants—helped in the drudgery of camp life, hampered in the long marches and harassed in the throes of wilderness fighting. Such were the precedent facts of the French and Indian War, pertinent as background to the main theme of our inquiry.

In annals concerning the exposed fringe of western New York, Pennsylvania, and Virginia, during the Revolution, and likewise in the French and Indian War that was its precursor, are recounted various episodes that cannot be authenticated, pertaining to the plight of women under conditions of utmost peril. If some of these incidents were hearsay tales, others were doubtless true as told. Most of these minor happenings involving border women at fort and camp had to do with friendly or hostile Indians. These outposts were often marked by the presence of intrepid white wives and Indian mistresses. Commingling of unmarried white men and squaws was already prevalent (long after Rolfe and Pocahontas), and in later frontier days in the Far West was to become so common as to be habitual.

The presence of women in the camps constituted a problem from the time of Fort Pitt and Fort Niagara to the days of Fort Sill and Fort Dodge—from the fall of New France to Custer's Last Stand. In the War of 1812, the land forces around Detroit and Niagara were attended by a scattering of camp women, both Indian and white. In the Mexican War much irregularity prevailed. Josiah Gregg, then whom none was better informed on the Southwest of 1840-48, declared in his recently published Diary that General Hunter's wife "was the only respectable female in the Army."

Reverting to the period of the clash of imperial arms between France and England when, in America, the so-called French and Indian War wrought havoc, the following is a typical incident, pertinent to our subject:

From Fort Duquesne the French commander, Captain Dumas, sent out a raiding party of some fifty Indians and a few French soldiers under Ensigns Douville and Corbière on March 23, 1756. The group in June burned the small stockades known as Fort Shirley and Fort Granville, and slew most of the too few English defenders. Douville was later scalped by Indian allies of the English, and Colonel George Washington, aged 24, sent the scalp to Governor Dinwiddie of Virginia. The wife of the petty commander of one of the gutted

forts was taken by the attacking Indians who, infuri-
ated by English eye-gouging of a minor Delaware chief,
tied her to a stake to burn her. According to the lone
and unverified account of the Rev. Claude Cocquard,
in a letter to his brother, a French soldier ransomed
her with his share of the loot, amounting to about
400 livres. This soldier, states the letter, wrote to Dumas
that he had rescued the most beautiful English woman
ever seen; that if his ransom money be refunded to him
he would surrender her. Otherwise he desired permission to marry her.

British camp women in the Revolution were an established institution. It was the tradition that men-at-arms
needed women-at-arms. Nor did the Revolution end the
British tradition. Wellington's army in the Peninsular
War (1809-14) had its share of wives and wenches—
forty to sixty in every regimental following, astride don-
keys, with scores, nay, hundreds, of Portuguese and
Spanish helpmates picked up on the road.[46] Concerning
these latter, Wellington, prior to departure at Bor-
deaux, permitted "a few who have proved themselves
useful and regular" to sail with the soldiers to whom
they were attached "with a view to being ultimately
married" (General Order, April 26, 1814).

And over here, closer to home, there were fewer of
the usual rout with the enemy in the War of 1812,
because it was largely naval. Indeed, when the British
came in Admiral Sir Alexander Cochrane's fleet to
sack New Orleans, some officers had their wives along,
and the latter brought their best frocks, for they told

one another that New Orleans was a lively place! The attack on New Orleans was repulsed, January 8, 1815, when the riflemen of General Andrew Jackson (and Lafitte's pirates) defeated the remnant of Britain's Peninsular army and deprived the ladies of their anticipated frolic.

Concerning the Revolutionary period, regimental histories preserve the names of the men; but the women camp followers remain anonymous, whether wives or otherwise. That we know naught of the fate of thousands of women who accompanied British troops in the American War for Independence bespeaks the dereliction of man. Even in fiction, the rôle of the woman in camp life during those fateful years has been neglected. It was not a taking over into campaign and battlefield of the vestiges of family life, but in common with all warfare a destruction of the ties and decencies of peaceful living. Let us draw the veil of compassion over the memory of these nameless women and call them wartime wives and brides of the barracks and the bivouacs.

The women who cast their lot (or were thrust) aboard British transports—whether married or merely estrays from the hearth—by their presence converted these hulks into bride-ships of a sort. In more than one instance they came over in contingents with the baggage—shiploads of women to share the fortunes or misfortunes of war—drabs of the dragnet. The question naturally arises what the hasty American army did in this respect, and the answer is presented—for the first time so far as we know—in a garner to follow.

# AMERICAN CAMP WOMEN
# UNDER WASHINGTON

## AMERICAN CAMP WOMEN UNDER WASHINGTON

IN THE long struggle for Independence the rôle of American womanhood was a prime factor of the outcome. In the spirit that led these women of the American Revolution to endure all manner of hardship, as in the variety and extent of their help, they did more than their share to bring the weary fight for freedom to final triumph.

Women helped make musket balls of their pewter dishes and molten pellets of the leaden statues of Royal George (42,000 was the yield of the effigy at Bowling Green, New York). They spun and wove cloth for themselves and the men in the ranks. They took over the farm work, from planting to harvest, made the grain into bread, and carried supplies to the troops. They kept shop and household intact, deprived themselves of finery, gave trinkets and plate to be converted into needed coin, made hospital supplies, and when near the scenes of hostilities, ministered to the sick and wounded. They brought comfort to American prisoners pent during the British occupation of New York in the Sugar-House, the Bridewell, and the Provost, or in the Walnut St. jail in Philadelphia. Enduring the insults of the guards, they kept many a captured patriot from perishing through foul and insufficient rations. Above all, as we shall see, hundreds who became refugees before the British advance went along with the patriot army, washed, mended, and cooked for the men.

Martha Washington was at Valley Forge in the hard winter of 1777-8, presiding over a circle of ladies in her sewing-room, and during other winters was with her husband at headquarters. The annals of the day recount incidents of how women aided in activities as widely apart as tanning goat-skin for drumheads or risking service in espionage.[1]

Soon after the first shots at Lexington and Concord in 1775, numbers of American women were rendered homeless, as always in localities overrun by enemy troops. Here and there in the environs of Boston there was a helter skelter exodus, beginning later in the day of April 19. Panic seized Ipswich, and Braintree was fearful. Cambridge and Arlington were sore distraught. A letter of that date shows the scurry: ". . . after Dinner to a place called Fresh Pond about a mile from town; but what a distressed house did we find there, filled with women whose husbands were gone forth to meet the assailants; seventy or eighty of these, with numbers of infant children."

But few went with the Minutemen, most joining relatives or friends in quiet parts of the countryside. Some women went into hiding with their children in the woods. It was not until later, as the months and years went by, that any considerable number of women joined their patriot men in the camps.

This is indicated by entries in the diary of Lieut. Jabez Fitch, Jr., an American who gave a graphic account of camp life in the besieging patriot forces around Boston. Six months after that fateful April 19, he wrote at Roxbury:

"Sept. 6th. I turn'd out at 3 o'clock, began to write to my wife but was obliged to desist in order to attend the alarm post. When we were there I occasionally mentioned among the officers Mr. Beckwith's observa-ion, (viz.) that before he left home he made a covenant with his eyes concerning women, but Col. Huntington replied that there was no need of that here, for he and Mr. Trumbull were yesterday oblig'd to use a spy glass to get a sight of one."

Three weeks later, he wrote in rather cryptic fashion: "In the afternoon went with Lt. Pease . . . up beyond the Punch Bowl tavern, to find him some white stockin'd woman, &c." [2]

As first commander-in-chief of the American forces (until March, 1776), General Artemas Ward, June 30, 1775, required at his Cambridge headquarters, "that all possible care be taken that no lewd women come into camp, and all persons are ordered to give infor-mation of such persons, if any there are, that proper measures be taken to bring them to condign punish-ment, to rid the camp of all such nuisances." [3]

There is evidence that two such women that year near the camp were prone to the oldest profession, and on February 10, 1776, in the Boston environs two lewd women were drummed out of camp.

Thus early in the war the problem was not too vexing for the patriot military leaders; but it was to become more so. When Colonel Israel Hutchinson was in command in Dorchester after the siege of Boston it was reported to him that disorderly women had taken up quarters in nearby deserted barracks. On June 29, 1776, he ordered inspection "that the Wheat may be selected from the Tares (if any be found)," and prohibited "Strolling that way after Sun set." The inspection by subordinates disclosed that women and children of certain men had gone there to be near husbands in the garrison. In an order of Colonel Hutchinson these women were "Cautioned against suffering any Soldiers coming to their Barracks at an unseasonable time of Night."

There were to be few military orders necessary among the embattled colonists concerning unattached women, but many pertaining to authorized women on the ration rosters. General Andrew Lewis, near Williamsburg, Virginia, July 8, 1776, ordered: "Officers of Companies are to return a list of the names and number of women they have, and whether single or married, in order to have them examined." [4]

Among American militia and the Continental line there were far fewer camp wives or other women than with the enemy. Many of the colonial soldiery, whether seasoned volunteers or raw levies, though married were footloose or homeless as a consequence of localities occupied by the British; hence uprooted wives often went along. Efforts were constantly made to curb irregularities and to keep down strumpet stragglers. The basic reasons for permitting camp women were not only that the practice prevailed among all armies, and the knowledge that quotas of women were with the British, but the inescapable fact that inroads of the redcoats had rendered patriot flight necessary in several areas, together with the natural desire of the women to care for their men—an impulse recognized by the American military leaders.

The officers usually condoned such proximity. But Washington was informed, November 12, 1776, concerning proceedings in a court-martial trial at Phillipsburg, New York, of Major Jonathon Austin, charged with cruel and brutal treatment of women and children.

Congress sent a Committee to Ticonderoga in November, 1776, to report on conditions in the Northern Army. As a part of their inspection they visited the hospital at Fort George, where there were 400 sick and wounded. The Committee reported these "suffered much for Want of good female Nurses and comfortable Bedding; many of those poor Creatures being obliged to lay upon the bare Boards. Your Committee endeavored to procure Straw as the best temporary Expedient." [5]

This relative paucity of women among the American troops contributed to the ragged, unkempt appearance of the patriot forces, chiefly due, however, to insufficiency of supplies and the hard guerrilla fighting of the determined men who disdained the fripperies and dress parades of the strutting minions of King George. Having too few women to wash and mend for them, the sons of liberty, said Benjamin Thompson (alleged

Tory spy) in his unpublished reminiscences, "not being used to doing things of this sort, choose rather to let their linen, etc., rot upon their backs than to be at the trouble of cleaning 'em themselves." [6] But even this needs to be qualified, for General Washington issued an order at Valley Forge that:

"The Troops are in future to be exempted from exercise every Friday afternoon. This time is allowed them for washing their linen, and for bathing." He added that no man was to be more than ten minutes in the water. Longer was regarded as unwholesome, and there were other orders to prevent men being too often and too long in the water.

The patriots were in tatters at Valley Forge because shoes and raiment to cover officers and men were lacking. The martinet British and hirelings, in cumbersome grenadier dress, were accoutred like popinjays, but to what avail?

Indeed, throughout the war the American soldiers never had enough equipment. A year before the last of the British sailed home from New York, it was announced by Washington in his headquarters order at Newburgh, November 26, 1782: "The Commander in Chief has the pleasure of announcing that a delivery of two shirts per man will shortly be made to the whole army."

But, alas, on December 23, the orders read: "The difficulties of transportation having delayed a considerable proportion of the shirts, which are ready-made in Philadelphia and which may now soon be expected, those which have arrived are to be drawn for by lot."

Officers, with pay too low to buy more than barest necessities, consumed their private means and worried over the maintenance of families at home. Colonel Ebenezer Huntington due to depreciated currency found his laundry bill exceeding his entire compensation. Writing to his brother from camp near Morristown, January 8, 1780, he declared: "Money is good for nothing . . . my Washing bill is beyond the limits of my Wages. I am now endeavoring to hire some Woman to live in Camp to do the Washing for myself and some of the Officers, th'o I am aware that many Persons will tell the Story to my disadvantage. But be that as it may, I am determin'd on it, if I can hire one on better terms than hiring my Washing." Some fifty officers at Valley Forge resigned in a single day because their families at home were not provided for. Washington, as late as 1780 disbanded the Pennsylvania militia for a time because of want of provisions, and in that order of August 20, communicated to Joseph Reed, admits "the deranged and distracted state of our affairs."

In the exigencies of camp life and marches the wives with the American troops may have been forced to neglect parlor attire, but there is no trace of dissolute abandon among patriot camp followers such as commonly characterized overseas armies. Nor was there widespread drunkenness; for (with some falling from grace) the Americans were intoxicated only by the prospect of new-found freedom from a rankling thrall.

Patriot prisoners fared ill at the hands of the British, rather from ineptitude and lack of facilities than through any inhumane motives; though Cunningham at New York was a sadist, and the prison ships were foul hulks.

British prisoners were likewise a problem with the new nationals. The Journals of the Continental Congress record that David Franks, agent to the contractors for victualling the troops of the king was permitted to supply British prisoners with provisions and other necessaries. The Journal for May 21, 1776, provided that such of the British prisoners as were not supplied by Franks, should be furnished with provisions not exceeding the rations allowed to privates in the service of the Continent. And, pertinent to our inquiry, there was this further stipulation: "That the women and children belonging to prisoners be furnished with subsistence, and supplied with firing and other things absolutely necessary for their support."

Three weeks before Washington marched into Philadelphia, and while encamped on the heights at Roxborough, a day's brief march away, he forbade any new women being permitted to become camp followers, and sought to get rid of all those "not absolutely necessary." In this order of August 4, 1777, he wrote:

"In the present marching state of the army, every incumbrance proves greatly prejudicial to the service; the multitude of women in particular, especially those who are pregnant, or have children, are a clog upon every movement. The Commander in Chief therefore earnestly recommends it to the officers commanding brigades and corps, to use every reasonable method in their power to get rid of all such as are not absolutely necessary; and the admission or continuance of any, who shall, or may have come to the army since its arrival in Pennsylvania, is positively forbidden, to which point the officers will give particular attention." [7]

On a sweltering Sunday, August 23, with Washington at their head, some eight or nine thousand men marched through Philadelphia, "down Front street," as Alexander Graydon tell us. But beforehand, Washington issued rigorous orders as to the decorum and appearance of the troops. From headquarters at Stenton, near Germantown, he that day ordered, in part:

"If any soldier shall dare to quit his ranks, he shall receive Thirty-nine lashes at the first halting place afterwards. . . . Not a Woman belonging to the army is to be seen with the troops on their march thro' the City. . . . All the rest of the waggons, baggage, and spare horses are to file off to the right, avoid the City entirely, and move onto the bridge at the middle ferry, and there halt." [8]

So meticulous was this order that it further required: "The drums and fifes of each brigade are to be collected in the center of it; and a tune for the quick step played, but with such moderation, that the men may step to it with ease; and without *dancing* along, or totally disregarding the music, as too often has been the case."

The men did as they were told; but not the women, it would seem. In what may be reasonably authentic description, one limner of the Revolution thus conjures the scene:

"They were spirited off into the quaint, dirty little alleyways and side streets. But they hated it. The army

had barely passed through the main thoroughfares before these camp followers poured after their soldiers
again, their hair flying, their brows beady from the
heat, their belongings slung over one shoulder, chat-
tering and yelling in sluttish shrills as they went, and
spitting in the gutters." [9]

This was doubtless the picture at its worst. Next
day the army was at Darby, across the new floating
bridge over the Schuylkill River at Middle Ferry, and
soon to plod its way toward Chester and Wilmington.
That day, Washington issued this order at Darby:

"The Commander in Chief positively forbids the
straggling of soldiers . . . and the General Officers
commanding these divisions will take every precau-
tion in their power effectually to prevent it; and likewise to prevent an inundation of bad women from
Philadelphia; and for both purposes, a guard is to be
placed on the road between the camp and the City,
with particular orders to stop and properly deal with
both." [10]

Human nature being what it was, and is, conditions
compelled Washington amid his trials at Valley Forge
to issue an order, February 4, 1778:

"The most pernicious consequences having arisen
from suffering persons, women in particular, to pass
and repass from Philadelphia to camp under Pretence
of coming out to visit their Friends in the Army and
returning with necessaries to their families, but really
with an intent to entice the soldiers to desert; All
Officers are desired to exert their utmost endeavors
to prevent such interviews in future by forbidding the

soldiers under the severest penalties from having any communication with such persons and by ordering them when found in camp to be immediately turned out of it." Or they were to be arrested for trial and punishment if "under peculiar circumstances of suspicion." [11]

A month later, he again calls on his officers for watchfulness, his Valley Forge order reading in part: "The General is informed that, notwithstanding the repeated orders which have been issued to prevent soldiers from straggling, the country round about camp and to a considerable distance is full of them." [12]

Perhaps it was too much to expect these men to remain quiet, with Spring whispering its harbinger, and a Republic to be sired. They had long been content to embrace privation for the sake of liberty, and to freeze at Valley Forge in pursuit of happiness.

Truth be told, the American patriots were too busy fighting and striving to survive, to hamper their protracted struggle with overmuch feminine ministration. Perhaps they were too near home! Be that as it may, those were less effete days, and the spirit that animated the ragged Continentals was shared by their helpmates, even to the point of taking up musket and cannon rammer. Indeed, many women of early generations had joined in the fights against the Indians during colonial times, and many in later westward days on the frontier had to take up arms on occasion in the defence of their cabin homes.

Mettlesome were the two colonial soldiers' wives (Sergeant Grier's wife and Mrs. Warner) who in the first winter of the Revolutionary War endured the terrible hardships of Arnold's march to Quebec, one surviving her husband who perished on the way (as depicted in the novel "Arundel," by Kenneth Roberts). Indeed, Aaron Burr took along his Indian mistress Jacataqua from Swan Island in the Kennebec River.

By way of digression it may be noted that "Louisa Baker," a native of Massachusetts, in disguise served throughout the War of 1812 as a marine on the U. S. frigate *Constitution*. Her real name was Lucy Brewer and after her honorable discharge she married a Mr. West and under the pen-name of Louisa Baker published a pamphlet narrative that had four printings in the last of which she gave her real name.

Moreover, women fought on both sides in the War Between the States, some of them disguised as men. Loreta J. Velasquez, a New Orleans girl, of Cuban descent, entered the Confederate Army under the name Harry T. Buford and rose to be a lieutenant. Another Southerner, Rebecca Stevenson, organized a women's battalion to avenge the death of her fiancé and fought valiantly in the defense of Chattanooga. On the northern side, Mary Tebe wore the uniform of the 114th Pennsylvania Zouaves when she served as vivandière with her regiment at Gettysburg. Dr. Mary Walker, garbed in male attire, while under fire operated as a surgeon, and was awarded a Congressional medal for gallantry. Mary Bickerdyke, herb doctor, ministered to the wounded with such ability that General Grant gave her a pass to go anywhere at the front.

In the War for Independence there were several women who took up arms, or in secret service and other devious ways aided the American cause. Grace and Rachel Martin, wives of brothers with the patriot army, held up a British courier and two British officers with despatches and sent the documents to General Greene. Emily Geiger, carrying a message on horseback from General Greene to General Sumter, was intercepted by British scouts. While a Tory matron was sent for to search her, she ate the letter piece by piece. When nothing was found, she was released, and delivered the message verbally to Sumter, as memorized for such emergency.

Betsy Ross was busy with bunting for regimental and other banners (though she did not fashion the Stars and Stripes). Lydia Darragh, living opposite the Golden Fleece in Second St., Philadelphia, during the British occupation of the city overheard enemy officers plan a surprise attack and, under pretense of getting flour, went to Frankford and warned Washington's army. Catherine Smith, the gun borer, died "unheralded and unsung" and was buried in an unmarked grave.

Schoolbook annals still acclaim Mollie Pitcher (really Mary Ludwig), who followed her barber husband, John Hays (or Hayes). She fired the last gun-shot at Fort Clinton before it was captured by the foe, and when her husband was killed at Monmouth she manned the field-piece where he lay and fired round shot at the redcoats. She was twenty-four and an expectant mother. Washington next day made her a sergeant and had her put on the half-pay list for life—or, as another version has it, made her a sergeant and gave her a gold piece. There was also Mrs. Margaret Corbin who, when her husband fell at Fort Washington at the upper end of Manhattan Island, November 16, 1776, took his place serving a piece of artillery, and who by resolution of Congress, July 6, 1779, received half-pay for life.

But most unusual was the exploit of Deborah Sampson who, having taught school for two years, in May, 1781, at 21, joined the 4th Massachusetts Regiment as Robert Shurtleff, and served until October, 1783, by the most "artful concealment" of her sex. She was wounded at Tarrytown and stricken with brain fever during the Yorktown campaign, when her sex was discovered. General Washington gave her a discharge from service and a purse. Massachusetts in 1792 granted her a small sum. Congress in 1805 voted her a $4 monthly pension which was later doubled. On her father's side she was descended from both the Miles Standish and John Alden lines, and on her mother's from Governor William Bradford of the Plymouth colony. As the wife of Benjamin Gannett she mothered three children, and was probably the first American woman to give platform lectures, her initial appearance at the Boston Theater netting her $7.

Such female combatants, whether or not in the guise of men, stand apart from the mere camp following wives, female relatives and sweethearts countenanced by the Colonial authorities in conformity with overseas precedent.

The extemporized American forces of the War for Independence preferred to skirmish in scattered formation when the terrain permitted, in contrast with the traditional massed tactics and volley firing of the British, having learned from open Indian fighting to seek protection behind tree and rock, to go light, shoot singly, move swiftly in small parties. Woodcraft stood them in good stead. But, until Washington welded them into a cohesive force, the militiamen campaigned as separate groups under autonymous authority, going and coming as they pleased. The Minutemen granted themselves leave of absence at a minute's notice; the strong Massachusetts Volunteers acted under their own leaders, and privates at first selected their own officers.

At the outset the armed strength varied from day to day. Some thirteen kinds of muskets and other firearms were said to have been in use by the patriots at the start. When Washington took over, the officers had no distinctive uniforms, and he ordered that ribbons or cockades of different colors should be worn. Soldiers in the ranks could scarcely use one another's weapons. If they had no musket or flintlock, no blunderbuss or squirrel gun, these first troops of the conglomerate army were directed to bring cutlass, sword, or tomahawk—even pickax or scythe straightened and fastened to a pole. The famous Lancaster rifle came later to a few and carried 150 paces farther than the British arms. The standard weapon of the English was the Brown Bess. After 1779 some of the Continentals had French Charleville muskets.

When Washington was appointed to take command of the raw militia, it took him eleven days in the summer of 1775 to make the journey on horseback from Philadelphia to the patriot lines besieging Boston. On July 3 he formally took command. Here he brought into being the little Continental Army, and here in addressing his troops, February 26, 1776, he said:

"It is a noble cause we are engaged in; it is the cause of virtue and mankind. Every temporal advantage and comfort to us, and our posterity, depends upon the vigor of our exertions; in short, freedom or slavery must be the result of our conduct; there can, therefore, be no greater inducement to men to behave well."

As the war dragged on, the army was welded, and the recognition of camp women as a collateral part of the forces became imperative. A routine grew up in this as in other matters. That discipline was instilled into the new Continental Army is seen by the orders. In the 2nd and 4th New York Regiments there were more than three hundred courts-martial cases from 1778 to 1783.

Washington issued some twenty-five orders pertaining to women with the forces, a number of these to curb riding in the wagons. The earliest requested count, at Bound Brook, June 4, 1777, required: "A Return to be made tomorrow, to the Adjutant General, of all the women belonging to the camp." [13] This is immediately followed by an injunction to the musicians: "The music of the army being in general very bad . . . exert themselves to improve it."

The first order concerning backsliding in the wagons, issued at Norristown, July 4, 1777, read:

"That no women shall be permitted to ride in any waggon, without leave in writing from the Brigadier to whose brigade she belongs: And the Brigadiers are requested to be cautious in giving leave to those who are able to walk—Any woman found in a waggon contrary to this regulation is to be immediately turned out. . . ." [14]

A week later from the same headquarters it was ordered:

"The tents of the whole army are to be struck to morrow morning at Gun-firing . . . with utmost speed . . . Women are to march with the baggage. Two days provisions to be cooked and ready this afternoon." [15]

At Wilmington, August 27, an order was issued which read in part that in view of early battle "every species of baggage . . . will now be stored . . . and our incumbrance on this account lessened . . . women are expressly forbid any longer, under any licence at all, to ride in the waggons, and the Officers earnestly called upon to permit no more than are absolutely necessary, and such as are actually useful, to follow the army." [16]

As part of the orders issued near Germantown, September 13th, we find, similar to Clinton's command to the British:

"No Woman under any pretence whatever to go with the army, but to follow the baggage." [17]

Next year, at Valley Forge, May 31, 1778, there were cases of smallpox. In an order of that day, the sick were to be left behind, and, "Commanding Officers of Regiments will assist Regimental Surgeons in procuring as many Women of the Army as can be prevailed on to serve as Nurses to them who will be paid the usual Price." [18]

The problem of wagon riding continued to vex. At his headquarters near Valley Forge, Washington's orders of June 19, 1778, were concluded with the following:

"The indulgence of suffering Women to ride in Waggons having degenerated into a great abuse, and complaint having been made by the Officers of the day that the Plea of leave from Officers is constantly urged when the Waggon Masters order such Women down: It is expressly ordered that no Officer grant such a leave for the future but the Commanding Officers of a Brigade or the Field Officers of the day who are to grant it only on account of Inability to march, and in writing." [19] Moreover, the General "is determined in Case a Violation should happen that it shall not pass unnoticed."

At his headquarters near West Point, Washington's order of June 7, 1779, read:

"The General was sorry to see thro'out the march a much greater proportion of men with the baggage than could possibly be necessary and that . . . the pernicious practice of suffering the women to encumber the Waggons still continues notwithstanding every former prohibition. The General recommends these matters to the particular attention of the Officers commanding brigades and that they will take the most vigorous and effectual measures to prevent the like abuses hereafter." [20]

The Pennsylvania Line designated the several small regiments furnished by this State as part of the Continental Army, as distinct from the militia. The Continental Congress was lax in providing provisions, clothing, and pay which was eleven months overdue, and at the end of 1780 the Pennsylvania Line reached the limit of its patience. Almost to a man they mutinied on January 1, 1781, broke open stores of ammunition and provisions, and marched to Princeton where they had a showdown with a joint committee of spokesmen from Congress and Pennsylvania. Promised pay, food and clothing (of which little was forthcoming), they returned to duty five days later at Morristown (Mt. Kemble).

During that winter the Pennsylvania Line there stationed comprised some 1,700 men, perhaps a third of the whole Continental Army. Here about a hundred women and children dwelt in huts with husbands who had only these shelters for their families. Joseph Reed, president of the Executive Council of Pennsylvania, and one of the above committee, had an anemic scheme to mollify the men; for less than a fortnight after the mutiny he wrote to the Vice President of the Council suggesting, with some condescension, a sop for the women who lacked decent clothing and who "like ourselves have their attachments and affections":

"A new gown, silk handkerchief, and a pair of shoes, etc., would be but little expense, and I think as a present from the State would have more effect than ten times the same laid out in articles for the men." He adds as an alternative: "If it should not be convenient or agreeable to the Council to do this, I will be one of a hundred to provide for one woman each, to be given only to those soldiers' wives who continue in the service. I have not ment'd it, lest I should not be able to effect it; therefore request to hear from you as soon as may be. I verily believe many of the men will do their duty better than ever"—if their wives were so salved.[21]

Reed was spared his contribution, for the scheme was negated, and the women went ragged.

Of the aforesaid twenty-five or more field orders by Washington concerning women with his regiments, just as the earliest was a request to know their number, so was the last; for at Newburgh, December 31, 1782, he stipulated:

"A Return of the number of women in the several regiments which compose this army, certified by the Commanding officer of the corps they respectively belong to, is to be given at the Orderly office on Thursday the second of January next." [22]

What the total number of camp following women was at this time is not clear, but in the National Archives a "Return of the number of women and children in the several regiments and corps stationed at and in the vicinity of West Point and New Windsor," dated January 24, 1783, gives the number of attached American women on the ration in that area as 405. That groups of women were shunted about is evident from Washington's order of August 22, 1781, at King's Ferry in the Hudson Highlands, advising the light troop detachment under Major-General Benjamin Lincoln "to take present opportunity of depositing at West Point such of their Women as are not able to undergo the fatigue of frequent marches and also . . . Baggage which they can in any wise dispense with." [23]

When his troops were to move from Newburgh down and across the Hudson to Verplanck's Point, Washington ordered, August 30, 1782: "No women to be admitted into the boats with the troops on any pretence whatsoever." [24]

There were perplexities caused by women coming from the enemy's lines in the vicinity of Verplanck's Point, both when it was in British hands and when it was won by the patriot forces. There were complications with several women taken as spies, and with wives of British officers captured on an incoming vessel. Washington even concerned himself in correspondence with Brigadier General William Smallwood at Wilmington as to payment for board and lodging of wives of British officers taken from such a ship. British women were among the Stony Point prisoners of war, and when an enemy regimental commander requested the return of two of these, Washington consented and ordered (at West Point, July 22, 1779) : "If any more women desire to go to New York, they are to be permitted without restriction as to number, on condition of their not returning."

There were various references of the Commander-in-Chief, in orders and in letters, to much needed provisions for hungry women on the ration or desiring to be put on the ration. Thus Washington wrote from West Point, October 19, 1779, to Col. van Schaick respecting applications for rations by a number of wives whose officer and soldier husbands were away upon the Western expedition: "This is a thing which I have never known to be allowed, and which, if admitted in one instance, might be claimed by the families of the whole Army." [25]

But it was the women actually with the troops who were a vexation. At his headquarters at Verplanck's Point, September 8, 1782, Washington wrote:

"As there are many orders for checking irregularities with which the women, as followers of the army, ought to be acquainted, the serjeants of the companies to which the women belong, are to communicate all orders of that nature to them, and are to be responsible for neglecting so to do." [26]

These excerpts will serve to show the tenor of the Washington orders. His patience amid the burden of difficulties was remarkable. Often he "recommends," rather than commands (though the day he took hold he "ordered forthwith"), and his orders were couched in wellnigh flawless English, even on the verge of battle, unlike the orders of some lesser generals, who employed, or whose transmitting captains employed, an independent phonetic spelling of their own! That good soldier and former carpenter, Capt. Daniel Livermore of the New Hampshire forces, was keen in combat with the "Britches" (Britishers), and would brook "no erregularity or Deprodations" among his men. Another cautions the "milishy, wimmen and chillern." On the

British side, ex-sheriff Capt. Caleb Jones of the Maryland Loyalist Regiment, notes (by way of sample) : "The Genl. is so Sorrey to have Occation to take Notise of the Sorrey Scanderlus and Irregular Behavier of Some Disorderly Soldiers."

The number of women attached to American forces varied considerably at different times and locations. A Return of those drawing provisions in several brigades and corps at New Windsor, in June, 1781, shows 137 women on authorized rations. A fixed ratio to men was never established, but excess of women several times led to official correspondence for the purpose of augmenting rations to care for them.

When General Washington conferred with Count de Rochambeau in June, 1781, on a concerted plan of operations, one of the matters determined was "the proportion of Women which ought to be allowed to any given number of men, and to whom rations shall be allowed." [27] The Secretary at War (Benjamin Lincoln) and the Superintendent of Finance (Robert Morris) had sought to limit total women's rations to a fifteenth of the issues to non-commissioned officers and privates. Washington, in a missive marked "Private," wrote Morris, January 29, 1783, toward the close of hostilities, noting that the "import" of the retrenching regulation implied on the part of the armchair economists that "an abuse existed, which required correction." With his usual wisdom he explained that this implication was set at naught by the circumstances he had confronted:

"I was obliged to give Provisions to the extra Women in these Regiments, or lose by Desertion, perhaps to the Enemy, some of the oldest and best Soldiers in the Service. . . . The latter with too much justice remarked . . . 'Our wives could earn their Rations, but the Soldier, nay the Officer, for whom they Wash has naught to pay them.' " [28]

In this letter from his Newburgh headquarters, Washington not only stressed that if a limiting of rations to women had been enforced, desertions of good men would have resulted; he further maintained that this feature of the proposed new system of ration issues would have cost more, and "would, if the strict letter had been adhered to, have involved particular Corps in great distress." He opposed a fixed limit, such as the proposed fifteenth, because groups of soldiers from certain regions had been rendered homeless. He cites, for example, "the regiments of [New] York, which, in part, are composed of Long Islanders and others who fled with their families when the enemy obtained possession of those places and have no other means of Subsistence. The cries of these Women; the sufferings of their Children, and the complaints of the Husbands would admit of no alternative."

In this, his only long letter on the subject, he assures Morris that the disposition to effect economies is mutual—"But if from misconception, mis-information, or a partial investigation, the interior of my business is taken up by others at a distance of 150 Miles, it is easy to conceive the confusion and bad consequences which must ensue." [29]

It is obvious that Washington felt irked by the implied criticism of factotums who sat in office at home, for about a month later, harking back to the subject, he wrote from his headquarters at Newburgh to Major General Henry Knox that military expedience had led to his disregard of the ration restrictions: "The number of Women and Children in the New York Regiments of Infantry before the new System of Issues took place obliged me either to depart from that System and allow them provision or, by driving them from the Army, risk the loss of a number of Men, who very probably would have followed their Wives." [30]

To Knox, former Boston bookseller who became so close to the Commander-in-Chief, the latter further explains the surplus of women with the New York troops who came from occupied territory, and adds: "But as that indulgence was to remedy, and not to create, an evil, I would by no means extend it to Women who on the prospect of it, have since been brought into Camp; and I would wish you to see that no such do draw Provisions." [31]

Washington's opposition to a fixed quota of women was therefore on the grounds that it would work hardships to some soldiers burdened with homeless families. It was not until three years after his death that the Subsistence Department was instructed, March 16, 1802, by an Act of Congress fixing the military establishment of the United States, to furnish ". . . to women who may be allowed to any particular corps, not exceeding the proportion of four to a company, one ration each; to such matrons and nurses as may be necessarily employed in the hospital, one ration each." [32] Such rations included, in addition to provisions, one gill of rum, whiskey or brandy.

A study of Washington's orders in the field reveals the dignity and true culture of the man, as well as his military sagacity. In a day when drinking was commonplace, he provided for the needs of his men. A Valley Forge order, April 16, 1778, provided one sutler to each brigade, who was to have "a Sutling Booth" and there sell liquors at a price-scale fixed in the order.

For those who could not pay, the same order provided also: "A Ration shall consist of 1½ lbs. of Flour or Bread, 1 lb. of Beef, or Fish, or ¾ lb. of Pork, and one gill of Whiskey or Spirits; or 1½ lbs. of Flour, ½ lb. Pork, or Bacon, half pint of Peas, or Beans, and one gill of Whiskey or Spirits."

Washington had written Congress, July 19, 1777, that the soldiers were inadequately supplied with rum, beer, cider, and soap. On the day after the Battle of Brandywine, Congress ordered thirty hogsheads of rum to be distributed among the soldiers in recognition of their gallant fighting. One wonders at the letter written by Major-General Alexander McDougall, from West Point, January 27, 1782, to Washington at Philadelphia, concerning the stoppage of rum issues to women and children, complaining of drunkenness and the insufficiency of the bread ration, which could be increased by reducing the rum issue. [33] More than once during the Revolution grains used for liquor were restricted to insure enough flour and bread. Rum and spruce beer were staple issues. Food was issued uncooked and meals were prepared over the campfire, often by the women who did the drudge work.

Care of the ailing was woeful. Six months after the outset of the War, a contemporary chronicler wrote, on October 27, 1775, concerning suffering in the camp at Cambridge: "Many of the Americans have sickened and died of the dysentery, brought upon them in a great measure through an inattention to cleanliness. When at home, their female relations put them upon washing their hands and faces, and keeping themselves neat and clean; but, being absent from such monitors, through an indolent, heedless turn of mind, they have neglected the means of health, have grown filthy, and poisoned their constitution by nastiness."

Latterly, when discipline was established, camps became more orderly and slatterns were expelled. But hasty retreats led to all manner of squalor and stench. At Hackensack, early in the war, pigs rooted in the piles of waste, women kept chickens, and the area was overrun with trulls. In disciplined camps most females sought to keep their men neat, but even here some threw refuse anywhere, and women and children neglected to use the privies, as indicated by occasional orders to enforce such use.

Trained nurses there were none, and there was no enlisted corps of hospital men of any kind. Occasional orders on both sides assigned camp women to the crude field hospitals or fort wards. Thus during the British occupation of Ticonderoga an order of July 21, 1777, read: "The Inspector of the Hospital having represented that two women from each Regiment will be absolutely necessary to take care of the sick and wounded, the Commanding Officers of Corps will give their directions accordingly."

Among the Colonial troops disease caused many more deaths than battle casualties. There was no set method of collecting the wounded, who sometimes lay unattended by other than comrades for days. Anaesthesia was seventy years in the future. The chief serious operations were amputations and trephining. Infection was frequent, and suppuration occurred in most cases. Blood-letting, emetics, blisters and nostrums were standard. The camp women assigned to tend those stricken or wounded were usually lacking in personal hygiene and had only meager acquaintance with the rudiments of healing. The choosing of them was haphazard and their service was desultory.

With winter ahead, the pinch of half clad men in tattered garb was felt. On October 7, 1777, ten days before the surrender of Burgoyne at Saratoga, the Battle of Bemis's Heights occurred. During the night that followed, according to narrators, stealthy forays were made by women of the American forces to strip the dead and helplessly wounded of their clothing, and to seek other plunder. This, it was said, made it difficult to distinguish the American dead from the British. During the engagement some of these women in strident groups were loud in lamentations concerning the fate of their

men, while others denounced the distressed with impre-
cations.

Near the spot where the British General Simon Fraser
fell, declares Neilson (who was so told by those who were
present), a pit was dug into which the bodies of forty
soldiers were thrown, "after being stripped of their
clothing by the women of the American camp." [34]
Other British and German corpses were hastily covered
with a layer of earth and brush. In later years skulls and
bones were turned up by the plough, and were made
into cairns on the field.

When Martha Washington joined the Commander-
in-Chief at Whitemarsh, some ten miles from Philadelphia, in November, 1777, she came through snow-drifts
in a rude sleigh. It was her first reunion in almost a
year and a half, and she tarried for a visit. Only Lucy
Knox was there. In mid-December the encampment
was shifted to Valley Forge where Mrs. Washington
rejoined her husband on February 10. She busied herself not only in wifely tasks, but assisted in copying
needed enclosures for letters or in transcribing copies of
outgoing communications for the records.

Conditions varied at Valley Forge during the six
months' encampment from December 19, 1777 to June
18, 1778. Moreover, the discomfort of wives of military
leaders, whether residing near or visiting the camp, was
far less onerous than among those humble women who
clung to husbands or lovers in the ranks during that
dreadful winter of unprecedented cold and privation.
Scores perished before the frigid months of misery were
over, with April icy and the river frozen.

Martha Washington, who had been the dominant figure among the ladies aiding the needy and stricken, retired to Mount Vernon when officers' wives were ordered to leave camp prior to the resumption of hostilities in mid-June. She rejoined her husband in the field during other inactive periods of the war. Plump Mrs. Knox, however, accompanied the Boston General on campaigns, and, despite her cutting tongue, became a close friend of Mrs. Washington who was later to consult her on the guest list for the peacetime Assembly. Mrs. Clement Biddle was with her husband at the Valley Forge encampment and other wives of officers daily filled the second-story sitting-room at headquarters, mending uniforms, sewing shirts, knitting stockings, dispensing baskets of food or home remedies to be taken to the huts of sick soldiers. And from homesteads in the vicinity farmers' wives occasionally rode in with hampers or saddlebags filled with bread or other cookeries for the hungry and ailing.

In the depth of that winter Lafayette wrote to his wife from Valley Forge on January 6, 1778: "Several staff officers are having their wives join them at camp. I am very envious—not of their wives, but of the happiness that this propinquity brings them. General Washington has also resolved to send for his wife. As for the English, a contingent of three hundred damsels reached them from New York; and we captured a boatload of officers' chaste wives who were on their way to join their husbands; the women were quite fearful that we might wish to keep them for the American Army." [35]

Others were at Valley Forge during or following the rigorous cold. From Rhode Island came, with her infant, comely Catherine Littlefield Greene, young bride of General Nathanael Greene, a boon for young Gallic officers with whom she prattled boarding-school French in her makeshift salon. There were weddings of bachelor officers or privates with girls of nearby farms. Other girls came from Virginia to marry stalwarts of the company of Old Dominion cavalry to whom they had been engaged. Some were billeted in houses, others set up housekeeping in crude log huts.

The Rhode Island chaplain, Ebenezer David, who was there, tells in a letter of February 3 that his missive had been interrupted to marry a soldier and camp woman "by virtue of General Sullivan's license." Apparently under wartime conditions, such authority was permitted to a military commander. Pennsylvania law at the time sought to discourage clandestine or common law marriages by issuance of licenses on a clergyman's application to the Secretary of the Province. Such licenses were not obligatory, but were intended for wedlock where the banns were not published or marriage in church dispensed with, to protect officiating ministers or others performing the ceremony.

Washington's day by day expense book in his own hand affords in its entries at this time a sign of the coming of spring after the winter ordeal. On April 10 is noted the purchase of a "mess of sprouts" and a dozen shad. Sugar and spices indicate Mrs. Washington was bent on preserving. On April 18 fifteen shad were bought and "1 mess of sallard", as well as four pounds of green tea and a bottle of snuff. Twice in June presents of strawberries were sent to Headquarters, one from a Mrs. Henry who lived near Valley Forge.

The following winter of 1778-9 at the army camp at Middlebrook, New Jersey, Washington was in the Wallace House, and Mrs. Washington was with him during most of the six months he stayed there (December 11 to June 4). General Nathanael Greene wrote a fellow officer in March, 1779: "We had a little dance at my headquarters. His Excellency and Mrs. Greene danced upwards of three hours without once sitting down. Upon the whole, we had a pretty little frisk."

In May, 1782 (seven months after the surrender of Cornwallis), there was a gala occasion at West Point when Washington in token of gratitude to his French officers ordered a celebration in honor of the birth of the Dauphin—Louis XVII. On Tuesday, May 28, Washington was "pleased to order a *feu de joie*" for May 30. A supplementary announcement on May 29 read:

"The Commander-in-Chief desires his compliments may be presented to the Officers' Ladies, with and in the neighborhood of the Army, together with a request that they will favour him with their company at dinner on Thursday next, at West Point. The General will be happy to see any other Ladies of his own or his friends' acquaintance, on the occasion, without the formality of a particular invitation."

An elaborate colonnaded arbor, 220 feet by 80 feet, had been built by many army carpenters and others working ten days. Though postponed until Friday, the fête came off with éclat—including military band and fireworks. The plan specified that after 5 o'clock dinner "thirteen Toasts will be drank, and each Toast announced by a discharge of Artillery. At half after seven the *feu de joie* will commence."

The festooned sylvan edifice enabled some 500 ladies and escorts to partake of food beneath its roof of interlaced boughs. A contemporary Gazette reports: "His Excellency, George Washington, was unusually cheerful. Arriving with his Lady and suite at midday, he attended the Ball in the evening, and with a dignified and graceful air, having Mrs. Knox for his partner, carried down a dance of twenty couple in the arbor on the green grass."

During the war Washington had headquarters in seven States, the last near Princeton. At Morristown and New Windsor, Mrs. Washington was with him for varying periods. At Newburgh the Commander and Mrs. Washington entertained Rochambeau and his suite. At intervals during eight years she shared the turmoils of camp life with her husband.

Prior to the War for Independence there had been among the Thirteen Colonies more clash than concord. Marriage of couples with the man or woman hailing from beyond the pale of the colony had seldom occurred, and then generally among the gentry. Among the plebian majority lifetime helpmates were usually chosen from the vicinity. But the war for freedom took the

Continentals and militia away from home, and the unmarried men in the ranks more often than not formed
temporary or permanent attachments with young
women in the countryside where the troops were
quartered for longer or shorter spells. Numerous resultant wedlocks brought about an amalgam among the
colonies facing a common foe which had not hitherto
existed and which fostered the new sense of national
unity that had been born by force of arms. Local or
sectional inbreeding was now offset by inter-colonial
blood ties. With belated achievement of Independence
after long years of struggle, the foundations of such
family life, followed by visits to distant kin, made firmer
the structure of new nationhood.

There were pangs for many in this birth of a nation
ere the camp women and brides of the barracks went to
more domestic firesides. The manhood of many a patriot
home was beneath the sod. Great hardships were
suffered by the wives and families of the Loyalists, and
many were uprooted to far shores who were of the best
blood of the Thirteen Colonies. The women camp
followers of both sides served their men according to
their lights. Over here the victorious Republic emerged,
for the experiment—still under way—of the great ven-
ture of 1776. May that hard-won liberty not perish!

++++++++++

# APPENDIX

++++++++++

## APPENDIX

Daniel Wier, Commissary to the British Army in America, made a Return, dated May 17, 1777, under this heading:

"Abstract of the Numbers daily victualled belonging to the British Troops, New Raised Corps and Civil Departments, including the Women and Children, Waggoners, etc., as by the Latest Returns to the Commissary General's Office." [A]

There are more than forty regimental or battalion entries in the tabulation. The grand totals are: Men, 23,601; Women, 2,776; Children, 1,901. Some of the entries follow:

| Regiment or Department | Men | Women | Children |
|---|---|---|---|
| Royal Artillery | 513 | 130 | 135 |
| 4th or King's Own Regiment | 388 | 80 | 50 |
| Royal Fusiliers | 264 | 73 | 84 |
| Royal Welsh Fusiliers | 370 | 59 | 62 |
| 26th Regiment | 305 | 82 | 144 |
| 27th Regiment | 365 | 80 | 59 |
| 28th Regiment | 327 | 70 | 44 |
| 38th Regiment | 355 | 78 | 73 |
| 64th Regiment | 436 | 67 | 91 |
| 71st Regiment | 1,274 | 119 | 83 |
| 1st Battalion Grenadiers | 707 | 114 | 69 |
| etc., etc. | | | |
| Totals | 23,601 | 2,776 | 1,904 |

These include 17 entries not giving women or children, such as foragers, prisoners, staff officers' attendants, absent detachments, waggoners, boatmen, and the like, comprising 4,440 men, so that the total of 2,776 women pertained to 19,161 men, not 23,601 as above.

Another Wier Return, addressed, like the above one, to John Robinson, Secretary to the Lords Commissioners of the Treasury, is dated Philadelphia, October 10, 1777. It follows: [B]

### RETURN OF NUMBER OF MEN, WOMEN & CHILDREN VICTUALLED AS PER LATEST RETURNS

| At What Place | | Men | Women | Children |
|---|---|---|---|---|
| New York ..... Staten Island .. Long Island ... | British Regiments | 4,084 | 1,407 | 1,383 |
| | New raised Corps | 3,530 | 306 | 245 |
| | Hospital | 1,000 | | |
| | Civil Departments | 352 | | |
| | Prisoners | 500 | | |
| | Foreign Troops | 6,219 | 233 | 31 |
| Rhode Island .. | British and Foreign, including Waggoners, Women, Children, etc., equal to | 4,650 | | |
| Philadelphia ... | As per Return No. 3, including Men, Women and Children equal to | 20,073 | | |
| | Totals ........ | 40,408 | 1,946 | 1,651 |

In addition to the above a number was left on Board Transports in Charge of Baggage.

Phila., 10th Oct., 1777

Since the number of women under headings Rhode Island and Philadelphia is lacking, the above total of 1,946 women is partial. A separate Return shows that among 3,619 male Hessians in Rhode Island were 118 women. There is also from the same source a summarized tabulation of the number of Hessian and Waldeck troops, which under twenty-three items and date of May 17, 1777, totals 11,192 men and 381 women.

Of the Rhode Island and Philadelphia ration figures (wherein women had one-half ration and children one-quarter), the victualling total of 24,723 at a ratio of thirty to one would indicate about 800 women. Adding these to the tabulated figure of 1,946, it will be seen that the 40,408 total of men had with them approximately 2,746 women on the ration.

An abstract of the numbers of men, women and children victualled at the British Commissary General's Office, Philadelphia, December 13, 1777, gives totals of 22,068 men, 1,648 women, 539 children.[c] Of the men more than 2,000 are tabulated with blank spaces for women and children, including the entry "Hospital 1,067." Thus the total of 1,648 women should be correctly compared with approximately 22,000 men.

Some of the entries in this tabulation follow:

| Regiment, etc. | Men | Women | Children |
|---|---|---|---|
| 7th Regiment | 359 | 44 | 42 |
| 17th Regiment | 406 | 67 | 30 |
| 23rd Regiment | 400 | 43 | 24 |
| 28th Regiment | 352 | 46 | 26 |
| 40th Regiment | 338 | 37 | 28 |
| Royal Artillery | 612 | 42 | 28 |
| Hessian Chasseurs | 738 | 41 | 1 |
| Queens Rangers | 494 | 50 | 0 |
| Maryland Loyalists | 147 | 13 | 0 |
| Gen. Shirbach's Reg. | 511 | 22 | 8 |
| Ansbach Reg. | 484 | 20 | 0 |
| etc., etc. | | | |
| Totals | 22,068 | 1,648 | 539 |

(A) Wier-Robinson Corresp.. Pa. Hist. Soc., Dreer Coll. MSS., pp. 8-10.

(B) *Ibid.*, p. 55.

(C) *Ibid.*, p. 81.

+-+-+-+-+-+-+-+-+-+-+

# BIBLIOGRAPHY

+-+-+-+-+-+-+-+-+-+-+

# Bibliography

## BRITISH CAMP WOMEN ON THE RATION

1. Henry Belcher, The First American Civil War, London, 1911, vol. 1, p. 335.

2. Allen French, First Year of the American Revolution, Boston 1934, p. 106, note.

3. *Ibid.,* Frederick Mackenzie Return.

4. N. Y. Public Lib., Mss. Div. (Revol. Troop Transcripts).

5. Jahr. der Deutsch-Amer. Hist. Gesell. von Illinois, Chicago, 1922, p. 256.

6. N. Y. Hist. Soc. Colls., 1879, vol. 12, pp. 373-8; 1916, vol. 49, p. 89.

7. Wier-Robinson Corresp., Nos. 1-3, Hist. Soc. of Pa., Mss. Div.

8. N. Y. Hist. Soc. Colls., 1916, vol. 49, pp. 84-9.

9. Max von Eelking, German Troops in Amer. Revolution, Albany, 1893, p. 262.

10. French, *supra,* p. 165.

11. Burgoyne Orderly Book, edited by E. B. O'Callaghan, Albany, 1860, p. 24.

12. *Ibid.,* p. 49.

13. Belcher, *supra,* vol. 1, p. 280.

14. Anon., View of Evid. Relative to Conduct of Amer. War, London, 1779, p. 43.

15. Belcher, *supra,* vol. 1, p. 335.

16. Mass. Hist. Soc. Colls., 1925, vol. 2, p. 451.

17. Roger Lamb, Journal, Dublin, 1809, p. 195.

18. James M. Hadden's Journal and Orderly Books, Albany, 1884, p. LXXXI.

19. Thomas Anburey, Travels through America, London, 1789, vol. 2, p. 224; Boston, 1923, vol. 2, p. 146.

20. Wm. L. Stone, Letters of Brunswick and Hessian Officers, Albany, 1891, p. 140.

21. *Ibid.*

22. H. E. Wildes, Valley Forge, N. Y., 1938, p. 273.

23. *Ibid.*, p. 278.

24. Geo. R. Prowell, Continental Congress at York in the Revolution, York, 1914, p. 232.

25. Madame de Riedesel, Letters and Journals, Albany, 1867, p. 125.

26. View of Evidence, *supra,* p. 77.

27. Von Jungkenn Papers, Wm. L. Clements Lib., May 10, 1778.

28. Roger Lamb, Memoir, Dublin, 1811, p. 75; Robert Graves, Sergeant Lamb's America, N. Y., 1940, pp. 248, 251.

29. Chas. S. Stedman, Hist. of the Amer. War, London, 1794, vol. 1, p. 309.

30. Sir Henry Clinton Papers, Wm. L. Clements Lib., Return for March, 1779.

31. Thomas Gage, MS. Orderly Book, Boston Public Lib., p. 102.

32. Wm. Howe's Orderly Book, edited by Benj. F. Stevens, London, 1890, *passim.*

33. N. Y. Hist. Soc. Colls., 1883, vol. 16, p. 595.

34. James A. Gardner, Navy Records Soc., 1906, vol. 31, p. 28.

35. Belcher, *supra,* vol. 1, p. 335.

36. Hubertis Cummings, Richard Peters, Phila., 1944, pp. 187, 194; Winthrop Sargent, Expedition of Braddock, Phila., 1855, p. 172.

37. Edward Braddock's Orderly Books, Feb. 26 to June 17, 1755, Cumberland, Md., 1880, p. 17.

38. Rupert Hughes, Washington, N. Y., 1926, vol. 1, pp. 206, 399.

39. Braddock's Orderly Books, *supra,* p. 37.

40. Col. Records of Pa., 1851, vol. 6, p. 426; W. H. Lowdermilk, Hist. of Cumberland, Md., Washington, 1878, pp. 135-6; Pa. Archives, 1852, Ser. 1, vol. 2, p. 348; Thomas L. Elder, N. Y. Eve. Post, Dec. 20, 1926.

41. Braddock's Orderly Books, *supra,* p. 50; Winthrop Sargent, *supra,* p. 332.

42. Col. Records of Pa., 1851, vol. 7, p. 342; Winthrop Sargent, *supra,* p. 258; Pa. Archives, 1877, Ser. 2, vol. 6, p. 530; S. Pargellis, Military Affairs in No. America, N. Y., 1936, p. 108.

43. Letters to Washington, edited by S. M. Hamilton, Boston, 1898, vol. 1, p. 185; Hughes, *supra,* vol. 1, p. 398.

44. Papers of Col. Henry Bouquet (1758), Pa. Historical Commission, Harrisburg, 1941, p. 78.

45. Dinwiddie Papers, edited by R. A. Brock, Va. Hist. Colls., 1884, vol. 2, p. 674.

46. C. W. C. Oman, Wellington's Army, London, 1912, pp. 274-8.

# Bibliography

## AMERICAN CAMP WOMEN UNDER WASHINGTON

1. Women active in Revolutionary War: Eliz. Cometti, New Eng. Qt., 1947, vol. 20, pp. 329-46; Grace M. Pierce, D.A.R. Mag., 1917, vol. 51, pp. 140-5, 222-8; Mary R. Beard, Amer. Through Women's Eyes, N. Y., 1933, pp. 54-87; A. M. Schlesinger, New Viewpoints in Amer. Hist., N. Y., 1922, pp. 130-2; Mrs. J. L. McArthur, N. Y. State Hist. Assoc. Procs., 1905, pp. 152-61; Eliz. F. Ellet, Women of the Amer. Rev., N. Y., 1854; Benj. J. Lossing, Living Men and Women of the Rev., N. Y., 1889; Wm. W. Fowler, Women on the Amer. Frontier, Hartford, 1880, pp. 121-49, 396-404; Susan E. Lyman, N. Y. Hist. Soc. Qt. Bull., 1943, vol. 27, pp. 77-82.

2. Mass. Hist. Soc. Procs., 1894-5, 2nd Ser., vol. 9, pp. 53, 61.

3. Orderly-Book of the Continental Forces, Wash., 1877, vol. 1, p. 10.

4. Orderly-Book of Gen. Andrew Lewis, Richmond, 1860, p. 59.

5. Orderly-Book of the Northern Army at Ticonderoga, Albany, 1859, p. 162.

6. Germain Papers: Rept. on Stopford-Sackville Mss., Wm. L. Clements Lib., Bulletin 18, Ann Arbor, 1910, vol. 2, p. 260.

7. Writings of Washington, edited by John C. Fitzpatrick, Wash., 1931-44, vol. 9, p. 17.

8. *Ibid.*, vol. 9, p. 126.

9. John Hyde Preston, Revolution 1776, N. Y., 1933,

p. 179; Dict. of Amer. Hist., N. Y., 1940, vol. 1, p. 279.

10. Writings of Washington, *supra,* vol. 9, p. 129.

11. *Ibid.,* vol. 10, p. 421.

12. *Ibid.,* vol. 11, p. 18.

13. *Ibid.,* vol. 8, p. 181.

14. *Ibid.,* vol. 8, p. 347.

15. *Ibid.,* vol. 8, p. 375.

16. *Ibid.,* vol. 9, p. 139.

17. *Ibid.,* vol. 9, p. 213.

18. *Ibid.,* vol. 11, p. 497.

19. *Ibid.,* vol. 12, p. 94.

20. *Ibid.,* vol. 15, p. 240.

21. Pa. Archives, 2nd Ser., vol. 11, p. 670.

22. Writings of Washington, *supra,* vol. 25, p. 496.

23. *Ibid.,* vol. 23, p. 38.

24. *Ibid.,* vol. 25, p. 94.

25. *Ibid.,* vol. 16, p. 489.

26. *Ibid.,* vol. 25, p. 139.

27. *Ibid.,* vol. 22, p. 203.

28. *Ibid.,* vol. 26, pp. 78-80.

29. *Ibid.*

30. *Ibid.,* vol. 26, p. 199.

31. *Ibid.*

32. Raphael P. Thian, Legislative History of General Staff of Army, Wash., 1901, p. 332.

33. Calendar of Correspondence of Washington with Officers, Lib. of Congress, 1915, vol. 3, p. 2026.

34. Chas. Neilson, Burgoyne's Campaign, Albany, 1844, pp. 180-2; Wm. L. Stone, Campaign of Burgoyne, Albany, 1877, pp. 66, 248.

35. Mémoires, Correspondances et Manuscrits du Général Lafayette, Publiés par sa Famille, Brussels, 1837, vol. 1, p. 99.

# Women in America

## FROM COLONIAL TIMES TO THE 20TH CENTURY

*An Arno Press Collection*

Andrews, John B. and W. D. P. Bliss. **History of Women in Trade Unions** (*Report on Conditions of Woman and Child Wage-Earners in the United States,* Vol. X; 61st Congress, 2nd Session, Senate Document No. 645). 1911

Anthony, Susan B. **An Account of the Proceedings on the Trial of Susan B. Anthony, on the Charge of Illegal Voting at the Presidential Election in November, 1872,** and on the Trial of Beverly W. Jones, Edwin T. Marsh and William B. Hall, the Inspectors of Election by Whom her Vote was Received. 1874

**The Autobiography of a Happy Woman.** 1915

Ayer, Harriet Hubbard. **Harriet Hubbard Ayer's Book:** A Complete and Authentic Treatise on the Laws of Health and Beauty. 1902

Barrett, Kate Waller. **Some Practical Suggestions on the Conduct of a Rescue Home.** *Including* **Life of Dr. Kate Waller Barrett** (Reprinted from *Fifty Years' Work With Girls* by Otto Wilson). [1903]

Bates, Mrs. D. B. **Incidents on Land and Water;** Or, Four Years on the Pacific Coast. 1858

Blumenthal, Walter Hart. **Women Camp Followers of the American Revolution.** 1952

Boothe, Viva B., editor. **Women in the Modern World** (*The Annals of the American Academy of Political and Social Science,* Vol. CXLIII, May 1929). 1929

Bowne, Eliza Southgate. **A Girl's Life Eighty Years Ago:** Selections from the Letters of Eliza Southgate Bowne. 1888

Brooks, Geraldine. **Dames and Daughters of Colonial Days.** 1900

**Carola Woerishoffer:** Her Life and Work. 1912

Clement, J[esse], editor. **Noble Deeds of American Women;** With Biographical Sketches of Some of the More Prominent. 1851

Crow, Martha Foote. **The American Country Girl.** 1915

De Leon, T[homas] C. **Belles, Beaux and Brains of the 60's.** 1909

de Wolfe, Elsie (Lady Mendl). **After All.** 1935

Dix, Dorothy (Elizabeth Meriwether Gilmer). **How to Win and Hold a Husband.** 1939

Donovan, Frances R. **The Saleslady.** 1929

Donovan, Frances R. **The Schoolma'am.** 1938

Donovan, Frances R. **The Woman Who Waits.** 1920

Eagle, Mary Kavanaugh Oldham, editor. **The Congress of Women,** Held in the Woman's Building, World's Columbian Exposition, Chicago, U.S.A., 1893. 1894

Ellet, Elizabeth F. **The Eminent and Heroic Women of America.** 1873

Ellis, Anne. **The Life of an Ordinary Woman.** 1929

[Farrar, Eliza W. R.] **The Young Lady's Friend.** By a Lady. 1836

Filene, Catherine, editor. **Careers for Women.** 1920

Finley, Ruth E. **The Lady of Godey's:** Sarah Josepha Hale. 1931 **Fragments of Autobiography.** 1974

Frost, John. **Pioneer Mothers of the West;** Or, Daring and Heroic Deeds of American Women. 1869

[Gilman], Charlotte Perkins Stetson. **In This Our World.** 1899

Goldberg, Jacob A. and Rosamond W. Goldberg. **Girls on the City Streets:** A Study of 1400 Cases of Rape. 1935

**Grace H. Dodge:** Her Life and Work. 1974

Greenbie, Marjorie Barstow. **My Dear Lady:** The Story of Anna Ella Carroll, the "Great Unrecognized Member of Lincoln's Cabinet." 1940

Hourwich, Andria Taylor and Gladys L. Palmer, editors. **I Am a Woman Worker:** A Scrapbook of Autobiographies. 1936

Howe, M[ark] A. De Wolfe. **Memories of a Hostess:** A Chronicle of Friendships Drawn Chiefly from the Diaries of Mrs. James T. Fields. 1922

Irwin, Inez Haynes. **Angels and Amazons:** A Hundred Years of American Women. 1934

Laughlin, Clara E. **The Work-a-Day Girl:** A Study of Some Present-Day Conditions. 1913

Lewis, Dio. **Our Girls.** 1871

**Liberating the Home.** 1974

Livermore, Mary A. **The Story of My Life; Or,** The Sunshine and Shadow of Seventy Years . . . To Which is Added Six of Her Most Popular Lectures. 1899

**Lives to Remember.** 1974

Lobsenz, Johanna. **The Older Woman in Industry.** 1929

MacLean, Annie Marion. **Wage-Earning Women.** 1910

Meginness, John F. **Biography of Frances Slocum, the Lost Sister of Wyoming:** A Complete Narrative of her Captivity of Wanderings Among the Indians. 1891

Nathan, Maud. **Once Upon a Time and Today.** 1933

[Packard, Elizabeth Parsons Ware]. **Great Disclosure of Spiritual Wickedness!!** In High Places. With an Appeal to the Government to Protect the Inalienable Rights of Married Women. 1865

Parsons, Alice Beal. **Woman's Dilemma.** 1926

Parton, James, et al. **Eminent Women of the Age:** Being Narratives of the Lives and Deeds of the Most Prominent Women of the Present Generation. 1869

Paton, Lucy Allen. **Elizabeth Cary Agassiz:** A Biography. 1919

Rayne, M[artha] L[ouise]. **What Can a Woman Do;** Or, Her Position in the Business and Literary World. 1893

Richmond, Mary E. and Fred S. Hall. **A Study of Nine Hundred and Eighty-Five Widows Known to Certain Charity Organization Societies in 1910.** 1913

Ross, Ishbel. **Ladies of the Press:** The Story of Women in Journalism by an Insider. 1936

**Sex and Equality.** 1974

Snyder, Charles McCool. **Dr. Mary Walker:** The Little Lady in Pants. 1962

Stow, Mrs. J. W. **Probate Confiscation:** Unjust Laws Which Govern Woman. 1878

Sumner, Helen L. **History of Women in Industry in the United**

**States** (*Report on Conditions of Woman and Child Wage-Earners in the United States,* Vol. IX; 61st Congress, 2nd Session, Senate Document No. 645). 1910

[Vorse, Mary H.] **Autobiography of an Elderly Woman.** 1911

Washburn, Charles. **Come into My Parlor:** A Biography of the Aristocratic Everleigh Sisters of Chicago. 1936

**Women of Lowell.** 1974

Woolson, Abba Gould. **Dress-Reform:** A Series of Lectures Delivered in Boston on Dress as it Affects the Health of Women. 1874

**Working Girls of Cincinnati.** 1974